Challenging McWorld

By Tony Clarke and Sarah Dopp

CANADIAN CENTRE FOR POLICY ALTERNATIVES

2001

Acknowledgements

We wish to thank several people who assisted in the preparation of this document with their comments, suggestions and expertise including: the students and young people with whom we've worked over the past three years; Lyndsay Poaps and Kevin Millsip at Check Your Head; Jen Anthony and Pam Frache at the Canadian Federation of Students and Karl Flecker.

A special thanks also goes to the staff of the Canadian Centre for Policy Alternatives who contributed so much to help make this publication possible: Bruce Campbell, Ed Finn, Kerri-Anne Finn, Diane Touchette, Erika Shaker and Erik Windfeld.

Thanks also to Studio 2 for the cover design.

Table of Contents

PART III   .....Canada & World

PART IV Methods & Tools

INTRODUCTION

More than any other single event of our times, the Battle of Seattle that took place between November 30th and December 3rd 1999 signified a new political moment in the history of youth culture and mobilization.

The thousands of young people who formed the human blockades at strategic intersections to shut down the meetings of the World Trade Organization (WTO) were, for the most part, highly organized and disciplined. They came to Seattle from points all over North America and beyond. Informed about the issues and trained in civil disobedience tactics, they came prepared to show the world that youth resistance to corporate-driven globalization had moved into high gear.

As it turned out, Seattle was just the beginning. The mobilization of youth resistance continued in Washington DC at the annual meetings of the International Monetary Fund and the World Bank in April, 2000; in Windsor at the meetings of the Organization of American States and Calgary at the World Petroleum Congress in June, 2000; in Prague at the World Bank meetings in September, 2000; and at the Summit of the Americas at Quebec City in April 2001.

Indeed, wherever the managers and architects of corporate globalization meet around the world today, youth activists are bound to be present. Between Seattle and Quebec City, however, the global managers had made significant changes in their line of defence. The chain-linked barricade erected at Quebec City, designed to protect the government and corporate élites involved in negotiating a Free Trade Area for the Americas, posed a new challenge to the protesters. Yet, if anything, the "wall of shame" served to heighten and intensify the desire of young people to come to Quebec City and join in the protest.

For Canadians, this recent manifestation of youth resistance should come as no surprise. In November, 1997, 30% of the 2,000 participants in the Global Teach-In on Corporate Rule at the University of Toronto (organized by the Council of Canadians, the Polaris Institute, and the International Forum on Globalization) were young people between the ages of 14 and 25. Two weeks later, at the Asia Pacific Economic Cooperation (APEC) meetings in Vancouver, hundreds of students and youth filled the streets in protest, and the international corporate me-

dia transmitted their stories and the pepper spray around the globe. A year later, during the worldwide campaign against the Multilateral Agreement on Investment (MAI) being negotiated by the OECD, the first major anti-MAI civil disobedience protest took place in Montreal, primarily organized by youth activists.

This was the crucible in which Operation 2000 was shaped and formed. Following the November 1997 Global Teach-In in Toronto, the Polaris Institute organized a project to enable youth activists to develop skills and tools for economic justice in an age of corporate globalization. The project was designed to focus on three main constituencies of youth: university and college students, young workers, and high school youth. Through Operation 2000, a series of teach-ins, conferences and workshops were organized, along with the development of several tools for popular education and action (pertaining to each of these youth constituencies).

Organizing on these youth action fronts, Operation 2000 has primarily served as a catalyst, bringing together diverse groups to work on a common agenda. Through this process, working relationships and partnerships have been developed with a variety of organizations engaged in youth education and action on issues of globalization.* Global teach-ins have been organized at Queen's and Waterloo universities involving all three youth constituencies. A series of high school conferences on globalization have been initiated at the Workers' Heritage Centre in Hamilton. Corresponding support initiatives have also been organized in relation to direct action campaigns of youth movements in Seattle, Washington and Windsor. And, in preparation for Quebec City, Operation 2000 played a key role in providing opportunities for young people to get training in nonviolent forms of direct action.

Challenging McWorld emerges out of the work experience of Operation 2000 over the past three years. The various tools developed for use in workshops, conferences, and teach-ins have been refined and expanded here for a broader audience of concerned young people and their allies. "McWorld" is the symbolic

---

* e.g., post-secondary student organizations like the Canadian Federation of Students and the Ontario Public Interest Research Groups, high school youth activities of the Ontario Secondary School Teachers' Federation, and the Ontario English Catholic Teachers' Federation, youth worker programs of the Canadian Labour Congress, the Ontario Federation of Labour, and affiliates like the Canadian Auto Workers and the Canadian Union of Public Employees, as well as youth initiatives of the Council of Canadians.

term we have often used in Operation 2000 to capture the new realities of corporate-driven globalization which engulf young people today. As author and journalist Naomi Klein has shown, today's youth live, communicate and act in a wired world of corporate logos, symbols and branding. The dynamics of "McWorld" provides us with a common symbol and language for both understanding and confronting the major issues of corporate globalization today.

The workbook itself is designed to provide some tools to enable concerned youth to develop skills required for *Challenging McWorld* in their daily lives on several fronts. It is divided into four parts. Part 1 takes up issues of globalization facing youth in both high schools and university or college campuses. Part 2 deals with issues and challenges facing youth in the workplace and in their communities. Part 3 addresses some of the major issues of corporate globalization affecting youth in both Canada and the world at large. Part 4 identifies tools and resources that may be useful in developing skills for research, education and action. This last section also provides a series of exercises and activities that can be used in working with groups on these issues and challenges.

Finally, in keeping with our opening comments (in keeping with the priorities of activism), we hope that this workbook will contribute to the process of building a national and a global youth movement to confront the realities of McWorld. Although Operation 2000 has been primarily focused in Ontario, working relationships and networks have been cultivated with youth movement building initiatives elsewhere in the country, such as Check Your Head in British Columbia. Similarly, Operation 2000 works with international organizations like A SEED (Action for Solidarity, Equality, Environment and Development) in Europe which serves as the hub for a worldwide network of youth activists. In many ways, *Challenging McWorld* symbolizes the basic purposes of these youth movement building initiatives.

PART I

EXPOSING
CORPORATE
RULE

ON CAMPUS
&
IN CLASSROOMS

1. ON CAMPUS

The impacts of economic globalization and corporate rule on university and college campuses are dramatically modifying post-secondary education. The democratic values instilled in a public, accessible system of higher education are being replaced by corporate-driven values of marketability and competition. Students are faced with the ever-increasing presence of big business. Developments, partnerships, and outright advertising and marketing may not seem noticeably different from year to year, but big business is there, behind the scenes, flexing its muscles.

Business interests have always existed within the post-secondary education system. In the United States and Atlantic Canada, businesses and foundations, like Rockefeller and Carnegie, were influential in assisting in the establishment of universities at the turn of the century. Corporations like General Electric offered land on which universities were built. And business representatives occupied positions on Boards of Governors. But the philanthropic motives of corporations and business interests have shifted and are in many instances suspect.

In the last 20 years, the role of corporations in post-secondary education has taken on a new form. The proliferation of business-driven governance, commercialized research, and outright privatization of programs, as well as intellectual property rights, are transforming institutions to the point where there is now an acceleration of private sector involvement in all aspects of higher education.

The particular issues confronting students vary from campus to campus: the struggles against the big five banks' roles in student loans; the dramatic rise in tuition fees and the deregulation of fees; the percentage of positions on the Board of Governors and Board of Trustees held by corporate executives; the commercialization of research; the proliferation of corporate partnerships and sponsorships on campuses, and the monopoly of food services on campuses by large transnational corporations—to name a few.

Underlying all these issues is the shift to neoconservative and market-oriented values in higher education and campus life itself. Each campus has a distinct culture, and for many students their values and priorities are solidified. However, campus culture across the country is being dominated by corporate-driven values and priorities. Universities and colleges, themselves, reflect the structures and ideologies of big business. There remains a danger that universities and colleges are becoming educational bastions of corporate domination in our society. For young people, the growing connections between campus and McWorld are becoming ever more apparent.

1-a. The Debt Wall

Since the Chrétien government came to power in 1993, $7 billion in federal transfer payments has been cut from post-secondary education. The provinces have denounced the cuts, but have done little to reduce the underfunding crisis facing post-secondary education. These cuts have had dramatic implications for students interested in pursuing post-secondary education across the entire country. Diminished government funding impacts universities' revenue and has led universities to seek funding from other sources, primarily through the private sector and through increased tuition and non-academic fees.

Student debt rates began to climb before the Chrétien Liberals took office. A Statistics Canada report on tuition, released in August 1999, shows that since 1990/1991 tuition fees for undergraduate arts have steadily climbed by 125.9%. During this time, undergraduate arts fees have more than doubled in every province except British Columbia, New Brunswick, and Prince Edward Island. In Alberta, the average tuition has tripled in that time. For the 1999/2000 academic year, undergraduate arts fees increased across the country on average by 7.1%.

With tuition fee increases in every province—except British Columbia, which has had a tuition freeze since 1995—students are feeling the pressures of post-secondary education in their pocket books, if they're able to afford it at all. The average student debt hovers at $25,000—$13,000 more than in 1990. In 1999, the provincial governments of Saskatchewan and Manitoba made commitments to implement a one-year tuition fee freeze and a 10% reduction, respectively. Newfoundland has also implemented a tuition fee freeze.

Coupled with increased tuition has come a variety of additional restrictive approaches to the crisis facing post- secondary education. None of them, however, has alleviated the burden that rests on students' shoulders and further limits accessibility.

Deregulation of tuition fees removes government guidelines and legislation for setting fees and gives universities individual control. Proponents and provincial governments claim that students who will be earning more upon graduation should pay more for their education. Severe financial constraints are placed on students, and accessibility is further compromised. Dentistry students can pay as much as $30,000 per year. At Ryerson, students in the new computer networks master's degree program will pay $20,000.

Grant programs that used to exist to offer financial support have all been scrapped by provinces, and the administration of the Canadian Student Loans Program (CSLP) was handed over to the big banks—the Royal Bank, the Bank of Montreal, CIBC, the Bank of Nova Scotia, and Toronto Dominion/ Canada Trust. In the deal every public dollar that made its way to the bank for student loans, the federal government offered an additional five cents to the bank, on top of the interest the bank earned from the loan while the student is enrolled. Not a bad investment for the banks. The banks also began to investigate potential 'customers' through credit checks, with the result that any kind of credit trouble would result in the denial of a loan (this last point is significant as it shifted the approval of loans from a "needs basis" of a social program to a more exclusive profit motive/ risk basis).

Apparently these conditions were not enough and the banks announced in February 2000 they were pulling out choosing not renew their contracts with the federal government. The

administration of the CSLP was contracted out to private service providers starting February, 2001. Edulinx and BDP, both won three year, multi-million dollar contracts to administer the CSLP—$96 and $46 million respectively. (Fifty one per cent of Edulinx is owned by the CIBC, the remainder by USA Group*— a private, for-profit administrator of loans in the U.S. which has actively worked to further privatize the American student loans system. BDP is a privately-owned Canadian firm on contract with the Bank of Nova Scotia for its student loans operations; BDP also has been contracted by British Columbia to administer that province's student loan program.)

In November 1999, the Ontario government moved to further cut education costs by denying loans to students with bad credit or students who do not divulge all their yearly income on loan applications, and by penalizing universities and colleges if more than 28% of their students default on their loans.

The Millennium Scholarship Foundation was announced in the 1998 Chrétien government budget as a solution to the debt crisis facing students. The foundation provides over 100,000 scholarships through a $2.5 billion endowment. Each year, until 2010, $250 million is allocated for scholarships. Eligible students receive on average $3,000 a year—of which $2,500 is taxable. Of the 80% of students who are in need of assistance to finance post-secondary education, the Millennium Scholarships offer financial assistance to less than 10% of them.

The cumulative affect of increased tuition fees and increased student debt is leading us ever closer to a system in which post-secondary education is available mainly to those who can afford it. The responsibility of these fees—and, more dramatically, the debts which will continue to be burdensome for years to come—are making university and even college prohibitive for many, but particularly for low- and moderate-income students who generally need to borrow larger amounts, which in turn take longer periods to pay off following graduation.

---

* USA Group has since been bought-out by Sallie Mae, now the largest financier of federal student loans in the U.S. Sallie Mae has recently filed a lawsuit challenging the constitutionality of directly-financed government loans.

Quick Facts:

▶ In 1999, the University of Toronto announced that it would raise medical residents' tuition. Fees for first year rose to $11,000 from $1,950. During that same year, University of Toronto president Robert Pritchard got a raise—a $25,000.00 raise, in fact.

▶ Undergraduate arts tuition in Nova Scotia leads the nation as the highest at $4,113 in the 1999-2000 academic year, followed by Ontario, where tuition has increased annually by an average of 12% in the last five years. In 1999-2000, tuition increased on average 9.6%. (Statistics Canada, Aug, 25, 1999)

▶ In 1980-81, tuition fees accounted for 8% of universities operating revenue, with government contributions accounting for 74%. By 1996-97, tuition fees accounted for 16%, while government contributions accounted for 58%. (StatsCan)

▶ In March 2000, the University of Prince Edward Island announced that it would implement a tuition fees freeze for the next academic year. Since 1990, tuition fees at UPEI have increased by 90% and student debt loads almost tripled. Students in some programs also face additional fees for tutorials and labs.

▶ A report released in August 2000 by University Scholarships of Canada shows that the overall costs for students attending Canadian universities are rising. Students attending Ryerson Polytechnic University pay $12,929 for tuition, books, and room and board on campus. Students at Acadia University pay $12,667, followed by $12,607 paid by students at Queen's University.

▶ The Millennium Scholarship Foundation's Board of Directors are appointed by Ottawa. Among the members are Jean Monty, chair of the Board, CEO and President of BCE Inc. and executive committee member of the Business Council on National Issues; Eric Newell, chairman and CEO of Syncrude; Suzanne Labarge, Vice- Chair and Chief Risk Officer of the Royal Bank of Canada; Micheline Bouchard, Chair, President and CEO of Motorola Canada Limited; and former New Brunswick Premier J. Raymond Frenette.

Discussion Starters:

1. What is the role of your University/College administration and the Board of Governors in determining tuition at your campus?

2. What impact has rising tuition had on your student debt load and/or that of your friends? What are your terms of repayment? When you graduate, how much will you owe in accumulated student debt? How much will you owe in accumulated interest charges?

3. What are alternative forms of financial assistance that could be or are being advocated? What kinds of grants or programs could provide debt relief to students? What distinctions could be made between students from low-moderate-income families and students from wealthy families with respect to allocation of financial assistance or student debt relief?

Resistance/Activities:

The Canadian Federation of Students' Access 2000 campaign mobilized students across the country, culminating with a National Day of Action on February 2, 2000, with events in 50 communities. Students demanded the restoration of $7 billion in transfer payments from the federal government; reduction in tuition fees and the elimination of user fees; a comprehensive national system of grants; and standards for quality, accessibility, and probability.   http://www.cfs-fcee.ca

A coalition of students, staff and faculty at Queen's University initiated a campaign to develop a Senate policy statement to guide the university in future policies regarding tuition. The coalition worked together to create a document titled "Accessible Education for Citizens and Leaders in a Global Society of the 21st Century." Initiated as a result of the implications of deregulation, the document proposed policies and recommendations that reflect accessibility, low tuition and public funding. In the spring of 2000, six months after the campaign began, Queen's Senate passed a motion endorsing the document.

4. What has been done on campus to raise awareness or campaign on the issue of student debt and rising tuition fees?

Resource Materials:

Missing Pieces: An Alternative Guide to Canadian Post-Secondary Education CCPA, Ottawa, 1999, 2001.

Hirtle, Benjamin *Dalhousie Inc.: The Corporatization of a University.* Nova Scotia Public Interest Group, Halifax, 1999.

Tudiver, Neil *Universities for Sale: Resisting Corporate Control over Canadian Higher Education.* James P. Lorimer & Company Ltd., Toronto, 1999.

1-b. Corporate Governance

With massive cutbacks in post-secondary education, universities are now more than ever opening the doors to the private sector, and corporations are lining up. Corporate donations in the forms of cash, equipment and services, and positions on Boards of Governors provide big business with greater access to institutions. As a former president and chairman of the Royal Bank of Canada put it, "It's in businesses's best interest to get themselves involved...in setting courses, setting the curricula so they get the kind of student they want."

Corporate donations allow big business to expand its presence and control within an institution through "charitable" donations. By making a relatively small tax-free investment in a university program or department, corporations bolster their public image of being "good citizens" coming to the rescue of an underfunded system.

Their generosity is highly suspect when lists of demands accompany financial contributions and outstanding corporate taxes are left in the balance. Joseph Rotman's contribution to the University of Toronto, for example, came along with 26 pages of criteria for the university to meet. The $15 million donation only cost him $6 million because of tax write-offs.

More insidious than donations is the role that corporations have assumed in governing the university itself. Until recently, the composition of Boards of Governors was a mix of faculty, students, alumni, and the community at large. While business interests were represented, generally they were local representatives. Today, however, Canada's largest corporations are represented with increasingly prominent roles. While the composition of Boards of Governors varies from campus to campus, corporate representation on many Boards skews the balance of power.

At York University, for example, the Board of Governors includes Marshall Cohen, past CEO of Molson's and director at Goldfarb Corporation, TD Bank, C.D. Howe Institute, and Barrick Gold; John Hunkin, President and CEO of CIBC; Barbara McDougall, former federal cabinet minister and director of AT&T Canada, Corel, National Trust, and the Bank of Nova Scotia; additionally, there are directors/representatives from Franco-Nevada Mining Corporation Ltd., Price Waterhouse, Trilon Financial Corporation, Bank Works, Livent, Noma Industries Ltd., the Fraser Institute, and the Business Council on National Issues, among others.

Corporate influence is further solidified and potential conflicts of interest arise when university presidents moonlight for the private sector. University of New Brunswick President Elizabeth Parr-Johnston, for example, also holds a directorship position at the Bank of Nova Scotia. While Robert Pritchard was president of the University of Toronto, he sat as a director on the boards of Onex Corporation, Moore Corporation, and Tesma International Inc. Most contentious was his directorship at Imasco Ltd. (owner of Imperial Tobacco, Shopper's Drug Mart). In 1999, a U of T report that measured how cigarette taxes translate into youth addiction rates brought the spotlight on the conflict of interest and prompted calls that Pritchard renounce his position on the board, for which he receives an annual retainer of $44,000, shares in the company, and monetary compensation for his attendance at board and committee meetings.

Corporate executives are entrenching themselves as powerful fixtures within the operations of universities. This influence deepens inequalities within the system and compromises the institutions' autonomy.

Discussion Starters:

1. Does the presence of corporations endanger a university's ability to protect academic freedom and autonomy? What is the impact of corporations's financial contributions on the University/College administration, on faculties/departments, and student affairs?

2. What "charitable donations" has your university or college received? What were the conditions attached to the donations? What kind of influence has been secured as a result? Did the corporations receive tax breaks for their "charitable donations"?

3. What has been done to publicly disclose and discuss the corporate strategies of Boards of Governors and fund-raising on your campus? What else could be done to expose the role of corporations on campuses and unmask their trail of influence?

4. What policies exist at your university or college regarding the role of corporations in governance? What specific guidelines or rules should be developed by the administration? What actions can be taken by students to push for guidelines that reflect the interests of students?

Resistance/Activities:

The Anti-Corporate Rule Action Group of OPIRG Toronto began the Corporate-Free Campus project in 1998 to expose, challenge and build alternatives to corporate connections at U of T. As part of the project, tours of campus examine corporate involvement within particular buildings, and the campus was put "under construction" to work toward corporate-free zones.

In 1998, students at York University launched a lengthy campaign to expose the corporate connections to the Board of Governors, and conflicts of interest within the university.

Quick Facts:

▶ The McGill Board of Governors includes John Cleghorn, President and CEO of the Royal Bank of Canada and director of the Business Council on National Issues; Paul Tellier, President of Canadian National and director of the Business Council on National Issues; as well as senior executives of Reitman's Canada Ltd., the Bank of Montreal, Silonex Inc., and Power Communications Inc.

▶ Sir Graham Day, Chancellor at Dalhousie University, was knighted by Margaret Thatcher for his work in privatizing and restructuring British industry. He is joined on the Board of Governors by Allan Shaw, Chairman and CEO of the Shaw Group Ltd., member of the Atlantic Institute for Market Studies, and a director with the Bank of Nova Scotia, Bank of Nova Scotia Trust Company, Montreal Trust, and National Trust; Ann Petley-Jones, Chief Information Officer of Nova Scotia Power, Inc. University President Tom Traves and Honorary Treasurer John Risley are also directors of the Atlantic Institute for Market Studies.

▶ The University of Calgary Board of Governors includes Business Council on National Issues Chairman and CEO of CP Ltd. David O'Brien; Ted Newall, CEO of Nova Corporation, and Rod Love, who is a former advisor to Ralph Klein (both while he was a mayor and as premier) and was an advisor to Stockwell Day during the Canadian Alliance leadership race in the summer of 2000.

▶ The University of British Columbia and Telus signed a five-year agreement in 1999 worth $4.1 million. Under the terms of the agreement, a Telus Mobility Industrial Research Chair with a $500,000 pledge was established, and funds were allocated to collaborate in wireless communications research.

▶ McMaster University launched its largest fund-raising campaign in the fall of 1999. The $100 million "Changing Tomorrow Today" campaign seeks "to support critical developments in the way we educate young minds, create new knowledge, and contribute to social betterment." The 'cabinet' that oversees the campaign includes Red Wilson, Chair, BCE Inc., and chair of the cabinet; James Alfano, President & CEO, Stelco Inc.; James Bullock, President & CEO, Laidlaw Inc.; Anthony Fell, Deputy Chair, Royal Bank Financial Group; Al Flood, Chair of CIBC; John Mayberry, President, Dofasco Inc. Other representatives come from General Motors of Canada, Aetna Canada, and the McMaster Board of Governors.

Resource Materials:

Missing Pieces: An Alternative Guide to Canadian Post-Secondary Education. CCPA, Ottawa, 1999, 2001.

Dowell, Blair *University Governance Versus Corporate Governance. Corporate Governance Package,* Toronto, 1998.

Hirtle, Benjamin *Dalhousie Inc.: The Corporatization of a University.* Nova Scotia Public Interest Group, Halifax, 1999.

Tudiver, Neil *Universities for Sale: Resisting Corporate Control over Canadian Higher Education.* James P. Lorimer & Company Ltd., Toronto, 1999.

1-c. Private Universities

While privatization of post-secondary education has been a topic of discussion for a number of years, events of the past few years and months have led to a much livelier debate. Proponents of privatization argue that they provide greater choice for students and can "reap magnificent profits." Michael Taube of the Fraser Institute wrote in the *Globe and Mail:* "We should consider opening up the marketplace to allow for and include private universities. By letting some students pay high tuition fees for a formal education, if desired, there will be more money in the total education pool for struggling public universities." (August 25, 1999)

The University of Phoenix operates in 35 American states, Puerto Rico, and B.C. It is the largest private university in the U.S. At the Vancouver campus, students pay $40,800 for an undergraduate degree consisting of 120 credits. Students attending a public university in B.C. pay $9,948 for the same degree over four years. The university was ordered by the U.S. government to pay $650,000 as a result of problems in its administration of student aid, including sloppy record-keeping and underreporting the number of students who had dropped classes. A number of jurisdic-tions, including New Jersey and Texas, have denied U of Phoenix access for insufficient library and faculty resources.

In spite of the University of Phoenix's attempts to woo Ontario, propositions up to this point have been rejected. But this could all change with the Harris government's introduction and passing of legislation to allow private universities to operate in Ontario. The Harris government has marketed itself as being "Open for Business." In April 2000, the government announced that public post-secondary education, too, would be open for business—open to privatization. Ontario legislation to permit private degree-granting institutions was quietly passed in December 2000.

Canada's first private online university is Ontario-based Learnsoft Corporation's Unexus University, which jumped online in Fredericton in October 1999. Following legal action by Unexus University in the U.S., Unexus changed its name to Lansbridge. Lansbridge offers both an MBA and Executive MBA and, as they put it, you can "get your degree without ever leaving your house or office...Anytime, anywhere: there's a university on your desktop." The two-year eMBA program is on your desktop for

$28,000. The university president is none other than Learnsoft CEO Michael Gaffney.

Queens's School of Business promotes its relationship with business directly on its website: "The Queen's School of Business relationships with the corporate community have proved essential to paving the school's way towards the 21st century. The 'Corporate Associates' program provides an excellent learning experience for the students, and it is a wonderful way for companies to know that students appreciate their gift. Corporations are also afforded an opportunity to make their name known to students who will be seeking employment once they graduate."

Students entering the School of Business faced $35,000 tuition fees for the 2000-2001 academic year, while tuition fees for the two-year Executive MBA program which markets to senior executives are between $60,000 and $65,000.

Whether it is a private institution or a specialized program, the results are the same. It is argued that private institutions are financed without drawing on public funds, but tax incentives have been provided to both students and donors of the institute; government financial assistance programs are available to students, and government research grants are also available to faculty. Additionally, accessibility is restricted, since students at private institutes generally pay higher tuition fees.

Quick Facts:

► *In 1997, David Strangway, former President of UBC, began planning a private, non-profit university. Planning has ensued, with bumps along the way, including difficulty securing land in the chosen community of Squamish, B.C. The liberal arts university, scheduled to open in September 2002, would offer "better schooling for those who can afford it". Enrolment would be limited to 800 - 1,200 students paying approximately $25,000 each in tuition.*

► *The Career Academy, a private college and at one time one of Atlantic Canada's largest private colleges, found itself in a financial crisis in August 1998, and unexpectedly closed the doors at 14 of its campuses. The announcement left students in the lurch and uncertain about the future of their studies.*

► *Keyin College's Charlottetown campus came under criticism from students in August 2000, as students accused teachers of being inconsistently absent, courses delayed by weeks, books not arriving on time, and having poor computer equipment. Ten of 18 students in the computer science/studies program had had enough and signed a petition asking the provincial government to take action. And if all the trouble from their first year wasn't enough, they were told that the computer science school wouldn't be accepting students in September. The Charlottetown campus is one of 12 campuses operated by the private college; in some cases, campuses are franchised.*

► *Carleton University sold its bookstore to Illinois- based Follett Higher Education Group in 1999. Follett has partnerships with 10 Canadian university and college bookstores, including Bishop's University, Champlain College, Sir Sanford College, and Lethbridge University.*

► *In April 2001, McGill University announced that U.S.-based Barnes & Noble would take over the management of its bookstore. This arrangement replaces the contract McGill signed with Chapters three years earlier.*

Discussion Starters:

1. What are the implications of private universities? What does this do to the accessibility and affordability of post-secondary education?

2. What kind of privatization endeavours have been initiated at your university or college? What terms and conditions have been attached to the agreements? What results or outcomes have you seen/discovered at your university or college?

3. What is your university's or college's Board of Governors/Board of Trustees or administrations' position on privatization? How does this position reflect (or not) the provincial government's position?

4. What actions can be taken or have been taken by students to draw attention to the issue of privatization?

Resistance/Activities:

In 1999, students and faculty at the University of Toronto, along with community members, launched the Free University. Courses are offered free of charge, on an ongoing basis, by a variety of activists, academics, and concerned citizens. Like Free Universities of the 1960s, critical analysis and educational experience are accessible for all.

Anti-globalization educators with Vancouver-based Headlines Theatre and Check Your Head developed and presented a live theatre performance entitled "Corporate U" in December 2000. The theatre event explored how corporations—richer and more powerful than most countries—influence our attitudes, relationships, economies and environment. The Firehall Arts Centre in Vancouver was transformed into a corporate university campus, and audience members were invited to participate in the action that ensued.

Resource Materials:

Bigge, Ryan. "Dr. Strangway or How I Learned to Stop Worrying and Love the Market." *THIS Magazine*, Volume 32, Number 6, May/June 1999.

Missing Pieces II: An Alternative Guide to Canadian Post-Secondary Education. CCPA, Ottawa, 2001.

"Private Universities: Privileged Education." Canadian Federation of Students' Fact Sheet 2000.

Who's Pushing Privatization? Annual Report on Privatization. Canadian Union of Public Employees, 2000.

Private Universities in Ontario: Decoys Instead of Dollars for Post-Secondary Education. Ontario Confederation of University Faculty Associations, March, 2000.

1-d. Commercialized Research

On university and college campuses across the country, commercialized research is being incubated. In his book, Neil Tudiver quotes a business executive in 1985 as saying, "Industry can no longer afford to do all of the long-term research it needs to survive; thus it is no longer looking to universities simply as an inexpensive source of trained people, but also as a vast reservoir of expertise which can perform that urgently needed long-term effort."

Through arrangements with universities and colleges, corporations demand access to publicly-funded research labs for their own private gain. Corporations sponsor research that can be patented, used to develop new products, and generate profit. The incentive to attract private funding becomes even higher when the private funding is matched with public dollars. Commercializing research not only underscores the market-driven orientation of universities and colleges, but also commodifies knowledge in the process.

The federal government, through establishment of the Canadian Foundation for Innovation (CFI) and allocation of public funds, consistently undermines the public education system. CFI money is available to researchers who raise 60¢ from a private sector partner for every 40¢ from the CFI. The 2000 federal budget provided an additional $900 million for investment in research infrastructure.

The Nortel Institute for Telecommunications at the University of Toronto is a win-win situation for Nortel. In exchange for the $8 million donation given over eight years, Nortel was involved in the selection of two research chairs, positioning itself to directly influence content and instruction, as well as seize virtual ownership of all research generated out of the Institute. Faculty and students were asked to sign over to Nortel exclusive rights to all research and inventions produced with Nortel money.

Private-public partnerships have directly led to the development of industry parks within the university campus, and to spin-off companies. Innovation Park, at the University of Saskatchewan, is one of Canada's largest research parks, with over 100 organizations located there. Some faculty have offices and labs, grad students perform research, and Commerce students can work on related projects. Business representatives work with students and teach courses. The management of the park is overseen by an advisory committee that includes the university president. This committee decides which companies to let into the park, based on criteria such as the company's links to the university.

In addition, Performance Plants Inc. was spun out of Queen's University in 1995. This spin-off company is one of 17 facilitated through PARTEQ Innovations, Queen's technology transfer office arm. The for-profit corporation has the exclusive rights to all intellectual property owned outright by or assigned to Queen's, as well as fostering partnerships with the private sector. Performance Plants has a team of 10 scientists pursuing commercial opportunities as they relate to plant biotechnology, with much of the research being done by scientists and students at Queen's.

Commodifying research not only privatizes knowledge by giving an individual or corporation ownership of an idea, but it also adds a dollar sign to the idea, commercializing the intellectual property. Students are brought into the process of commercializing research as workers for private gain in its crudest form, requiring them to pay (through tuition) to perform private research. Students have been forced to sign confidentiality agreements, essentially imposing gag orders on them.

Commercialization of research implies marketability, which in turn creates further risks that the humanities, already underfunded, will receive even less public funding. Emphasis is put only on medical and applied science, not the economic, social and political research of the humanities. Additionally, private funding should not be seen as a replacement for direct government funding for universities and colleges.

Quick Facts:

▶ *54% of all faculty teach humanities and social sciences, but only 20% of the Canada Research Chairs are allocated to these disciplines. The natural sciences and engineering account for 29% of faculty, while they receive 45% of the chairs.*

▶ *In 1995, UBC awarded a grant to develop Web Course Tools "as a way to apply innovative technologies to facilitate course preparation and enrich students' learning experiences." Two years later, it was launched commercially, and today it boasts accounts with 1,494 institutions in 57 countries.*

▶ *While he was Chancellor of Concordia, Francesco Bellini's BioChem Pharma Inc. donated $1.8 million to the university. The gift was matched by the CFI and the provincial government and went toward the establishment of the BioChem Pharma Genomics Facility.*

▶ *At the University of Regina, Canadian Occidental Petroleum Inc. contributed $1 million towards the building of a new Petroleum Technology Research Centre. The centre received an additional $26.5 million in public funds.*

▶ *Bell Canada's $13.5 million donation to U of T in 1999 established the Bell Canada University Labs, along with four new research chairs.*

Resource Materials:

"How Ottawa is Weakening PSE." *CAUT Now!* Volume 2, Number 5 June 21, 2000.

Missing Pieces II: An Alternative Guide to Canadian Post-Secondary Education. CCPA, Ottawa, 2001.

Panzanno, Linda "Masters of the University." *The Coast*, Halifax, September 9, 1999.

Shaker, Erika; Doherty-Delorme, Denise. "Higher Education, Limited. Private Money, Private Agendas." *Education Limited*, Volume 1 Number 4, Spring, 1999.

Turk, James L. (ed.) *The Corporate Campus: Commercialization and the Dangers to Canada's Colleges and Universities.* James Lorimer and Company Ltd., Toronto, 2000.

Discussion Starters:

1. What is the role of university and college presidents in preserving institutional autonomy and academic freedom?

2. Have there been noticeable differences in the way information is imparted or changes within your university/college since partnerships were formed? What are the implications of private-public partnerships on students, faculty, staff, and the institution as a whole?

3. What sort of action can be taken to unmask the big business partnerships and the criteria for such projects in your university or college?

4. Are there guidelines surrounding commercialization that exist at your university or college? What sort of guidelines would protect faculty, students, and the public interest of knowledge?

1-e. Advertising

Corporate intrusion, such as advertising and exclusivity deals, have become tangible rallying points for students trying to fight back against commercialization and branding.

Campuses are one obvious example. Since the 1990s, Canadian campuses have been a major battleground for the Pepsi-vs-Coca-Cola wars. Initially, student debates tend to focus on the limited choice, volume and placement of vending machines, but beneath the surface lie deeper and more profound issues of concern.

These exclusivity deals are lucrative. For the corporations, it brings them closer to their market and raises their profile, not to mention their profits. The agreements also infuse money into student unions and the university itself, again underlying just how cash-strapped universities are. Additionally, beyond the bottom line of the finances, the agreements are secretive, which in many cases is the most contentious aspect. The University of British Columbia, while negotiating its contract, for example, argued that making the terms and conditions known before the deal was signed could have jeopardized the agreement itself and opened the company up to competition. Five years after the agreement was signed, however, students still don't know what's in it.

In mid-October, 1999, McGill students wandering through the new Student Services Building encountered the Coca-Cola International Students Lounge, the public recognition for Coke's donation to the university. By the winter, students launched an aggressive campaign to keep the 11-year, $10 million Coke deal out of their campus. Contained within the secretive agreement was a quota, essentially promising that McGill students would consume a specific amount of Coke products or the university would face a penalty. Following a referendum in which 54% of students who participated rejected the deal, the administration announced it would no longer pursue "the real thing."

Coca-Cola and rival PepsiCo are not the only transnational corporations jockeying to serve on campus. Marriott and Aramark, both U.S.-based corporations, have exclusivity deals with Canadian colleges and universities to provide food services.

Zoom Media advertises in the washrooms at more than 70 colleges and universities across Canada. At Concordia, Zoom Media has 280 washroom ad spaces, of which 10% are given to the university for department and student notices. In the spring of 2000, students had had enough and wanted to be able to "pee freely." The Concordia Student Union held a vote to ask students whether or not Zoom Media should give the majority of ad spaces to the student union. Six out of 10 (61%) of students voted in favour. The University of Montreal also announced it would not renew its contract with Zoom Media.

Between the vending machines, food courts, washroom ads and merchandise, not to mention corporate logos on buildings and rooms, there is virtually no space that has not been taken over by advertising.

Quick Facts:

▶ *Carleton University magazine announced in the winter of 2000 that washrooms on campus could soon be adorned with interactive and three-dimensional electronic ads. The most recent development in washroom advertising by Zoom Media requires approval by the university.*

▶ *When UBC and Capilano College signed deals with Coke, the student newspapers, The Ubyssey and The Capilano Courier, filed a Freedom of Information request to have the contract disclosed. The Freedom of Information Commissioner released just three pages. The Ubyssey and The Courier appealed, and in May 2001 the B.C. Information and Privacy Commissioner ruled that the contracts are public documents. Lawyers for the schools were given 30 days to seek an appeal, and, failing that, the dollar amounts contained in the contracts would have to be made public.*

▶ *The proposed contract with Coca-Cola at the Université Québec à Montréal included a clause which ensured that consumption of Coke would increase by 130% over 10 years, failing which the contract would be renewed for two years at no cost to Coke.*

▶ *In the spring of 1999, six Capilano College students applied for a federal review of their school's monopoly deal with Coca-Cola, claiming that the deal violates the Competition Act.*

Discussion Starters:

1. Do principles and/or guidelines exist at your university/college to govern commercial marketing to students? What are included in the guidelines? If they don't exist, what principles should be included in such agreements or guidelines?

2. What kind of corporate advertising exists within your campus? What is the relationship between the company and the university/college? In exchange for advertising/marketing space within the school, what is given to the corporation in return?

3. What actions have been taken by students to promote discussion and take action?

Resistance/Activities:

Student-led campaigns targeting companies not only expose the details facing the campus, but also broaden the scope to focus on issues that affect the whole community. Students Against Sweatshops campaigns on several Canadian campuses, for example, raise awareness of sweatshop issues and pressure their schools to adopt codes of conduct governing the production and purchase of their schools' clothing.

In March 2000, students at U of T occupied President Pritchard's office for 10 days to put pressure on the university to adopt a code of conduct on university purchasing practices. The code included a requirement that workers producing U of T merchandise be paid a living wage. In May, the governing council finally adopted the student-backed new licensing policy and code of conduct.

Resource Materials:

Klein, Naomi. *No Logo*, Knopf Canada, Toronto, 2000.

Students Campaign for Sweat-free Campus, Maquila Solidarity Network, February 1999.

Santos, Genny. "No Sweat! Anti-Sweatshop Campuses on the go," *The Student Activist*, September 1999.

Schmidt, Sarah. "U of You Name It," *THIS Magazine*, Sept/Oct. 1998.

Shaker, Erika "Growing the Market: Of Urinals and University Centres - targeting the campus crowd," *Missing Pieces II: An Alternative Guide to Canadian Post-Secondary Education*. CCPA, Ottawa, 2001.

2. IN CLASSROOMS

Corporate presence continues to creep into the classrooms of public schools, as well. Government restructuring across the country is reshaping the public education system, opening the doors ever wider to corporate interests. Cash-strapped schools are increasingly turning to the private sector to form business-school partnerships. Corporations are eager to provide the much- needed equipment, services and resources, while schools ensure a captive audience for the marketing of products.

Ready or not, students become immersed in the corporate-dominated culture of market values and priorities as soon as they walk through the doors. The marketing strategies of corporations have targeted high school and elementary school students as consumers, both inside the classroom and out.

Corporate logos and brand name products are now prominently placed throughout most schools—everywhere from the gym floor to the cafeteria to the textbooks from which students learn. Beverage companies like Coke and Pepsi sign exclusive deals with school boards, and sponsor rallies over lunch hours. Corporations are now sponsoring entire schools in some communities.

Even the curriculum is not out of the reach of private interests. Corporate curriculum integrating logos and products are making their way into textbooks and through business-developed supplemental materials.

But as the profit-driven intrusion of big business increases and governments correspondingly underfund and withdraw from the public system, students themselves are beginning to challenge this corporate takeover of education. They are educating and organizing themselves around these issues that fundamentally affect their education, and are channelling their energies toward taking action. In the minds of many students, the connection between government "restructuring" and the invasion of big business is becoming more and more clear.

2-a. Education Restructuring

From coast to coast, students and teachers have been under attack. Education restructuring or 'reforms' have been intensifying since the late 1970s. We have been told by politicians, business lobbies and right-wing think-tanks that the education system is failing. As a result, there has been a growing assault on our public school system through the proliferation of private-public partnerships, the contracting-out of services such as janitorial and food, and in some cases outright privatization.

Public education is undergoing a dangerous transformation. The manifestations may appear to differ from province to province, but the consequences remain the same: underfunding the education system, concentrating power in the hands of provincial governments, and opening up public schools to private interests.

These "reforms" have been touted as improvements that offer students and their parents greater choice. In Alberta, the Klein government initially took the lead enthusiastically, redefining education in the province through legislated reforms. The reforms included increased funding for private schools, the creation of school councils, the consolidation of school boards, the introduction of a voucher system, and the establishment of charter schools. Today, Alberta schools are indeed "open for business."

Ontario's Harris government, having declared the entire province to be "open for business," moved swiftly to bring the Alberta reforms to Ontario. But Ontario added another twist. According to a report released in June 2001, funding on a real per-pupil basis has been reduced by almost $2.3 billion since 1995. Class size has continually risen, with some classes now as large as 35 students, in some cases even as large as 42 or even 50 students.

Bill upon bill has radically remodelled Ontario's education system. The Education Quality Improvement Act (Bill 160) gutted teachers' collective bargaining rights, weakened school boards' authority, and eliminated the checks and balances of governance for the system.

The Education Accountability Act (Bill 74), further restricts teachers' collective bargaining rights, increases teachers' class loads, and therefore reduces the amount of time teachers will be able to spend with students. It also sought to make extracurricular activities mandatory. Standardized testing for students, along with teacher testing, further changes the sys-

tem. And the latest addition of a tax credit put directly into the hands of parents whose children attend private schools takes money away from the system and signals yet another shift away from publicly-funded education.

In Nova Scotia, the introduction of a private-public partnerships program (P3) signalled another new Canadian development: the private construction of public schools. Private developers construct and furnish the school, providing everything from desks to blackboards, phones to computers. The public system is reduced to supplying the administration, the teachers, and the students.

The experience in Nova Scotia has been costly. While the original plan would, in theory, save the government money, P3s have in fact cost more than they would have cost had they been financed publicly. Though the school itself is leased to the private sector, the public still pays for maintenance of what should be a public asset. Corporate interests have guided the development of schools, including their location.

Corporate interests have been keen to "help" the system earn a passing grade. Offering "business" solutions to make schools more competitive and equip students for the workforce have given governments the "right" direction in which to proceed. The end result is pushing us closer to a two-tiered education system.

Quick Facts:

► Canada spends on average $4,715 per student, compared to the $7,381 spent per student in the United States. The average per-student expenditure of Canada's 10 provinces falls below those of 48 of the 50 American states.

► New Brunswick eliminated school boards, centralizing decision-making power within the Department of Education. Every other province has reduced or amalgamated the number of school boards, thus providing opportunities for community-based citizen participation in our education system.

► Between 1993 and 1997, 42 schools were closed in Saskatchewan, 37 of them rural schools. Over 130 Ontario schools were closed in 1999 or are slated be to closed in the near future.

► Evergreen Park is New Brunswick's first P3; according to the New Brunswick Auditor, the school cost $900,000 more to build than it would have cost had the province taken it on. The province is paying another $421,000 over the 25-year lease to lease back the land it sold to the Greenarm corporation for $275,000.

► At present, Alberta has 10 charter schools. Of the original charter schools that opened, two were closed, two were taken over by the government or local school boards, and in one case criminal fraud was found to have been committed by members involved with the Charter school.

Discussion Starters:

1. How have the impacts of education restructuring affected your school and classes? How are the decisions made by provincial governments being manifested on a local level?

2. What noticeable changes have you witnessed within your school and within the school board? What does this say about the quality of public education in your community?

3. What are the social consequences of the deteriorating quality of public education? How does a weaker public education system provide incentives for the creation of more private institutions for education?

4. What actions can or have been taken to raise awareness about the impacts of education restructuring? What actions could be taken in your community by students, teachers and/or parents?

Resistance/Activities:

When the Harris government celebrated the new millennium by producing a book called "My Ontario," Ottawa high school students sparked a province-wide resistance by organizing a mass return of the books to Queen's Park. Buses were rented by students to take the books back to Toronto. Students argued that the money spent on the books could have been better spent on the education system itself. In total, over 11,000 books were dumped at Queen's Park.

In the spring of 2000, Nova Scotians organized rallies, demonstrations, and walk-outs from high schools to protest the Lord government's announcement that nearly $27 million was to be cut from education. For several consecutive days, students marched with their teachers and parents in opposition to this gutting of the public school system.

Resource Materials:

Barlow, Maude and Robertson, Heather-jane. *Class Warfare: The Assault on Canada's Schools.* Key Porter, Toronto, 1994.

Who's Pushing Privatization? Annual Report on Privatization Canadian Union of Public Employees, 2000.

Mackenzie, Hugh. "Manufactured Crisis: A Report Card on Ontario's 'Student-Focused Funding' Formula." *Ontario Alternative Budget Paper #13*, CCPA, June 2001.

McEwen, John. "Provinces' school spending still far below most U.S. states," *CCPA Education Monitor*, Volume 4, Number 1, Winter 2000.

2-b. Business Education Partnerships

In recent years, business-school partnerships have mushroomed in the public education system across Canada. According to the National Business and Education Centre of the Conference Board of Canada, there are more than 20,000 of them in place across Canada.

These business-school partnerships have emerged to fill the void created by government cutbacks. The question that must be asked, however, is: whose interests are ultimately served by these partnerships? The students? School boards? Or the private sector? The evidence to date shows that students are not the main beneficiaries. Indeed, students who protest against these partnerships are often punished.

In the U.S., for example, a student in Georgia was suspended from school in 1998 for wearing a Pepsi shirt on "Coke Day." And, closer to home, in Mississauga, during "Meadowstock," the Battle of the Bands contest, a member of one band, wearing a "YNN stinks" T-shirt, engaged the audience in a dialogue about YNN, asking what they thought of it. The audience booed. The performance was stopped, the band was informed that they had been disqualified.

These corporations may provide financially starved schools with a variety of costly supplies, equipment and services, but they also get an enormous bargain in return: a captive audience, a market, considerable public recognition for their "social philanthropy," and free use of teachers as credible corporate spokespersons—not to mention legitimizing a corporate presence in the school environment.

Take, for example, the Campbell Soup Company's nutrition program, "Feeding our Future," which was launched in partnership with the Toronto District School Board. The company began its program by offering soup to students at lunch to supplement the lunches students bring from home. Campbell's also helped to found the Toronto Foundation for Student Success, a foundation that provides nutritional programs in Toronto schools, as well as free equipment and financial support.

The rate at which business/education partnerships are being established with public schools, and the terms and conditions of the contracts, are deeply disconcerting. In the fall of 1999, Wal-Mart Canada announced its adopt-a-school program. Under the program, Wal-Mart stores sponsor or "adopt" a local elementary or secondary school in their community. The "adoption" lasts for a one-year period, after which the stores have the option of renewing their adoption. Wal-Mart boasts that all of its stores are participating in the program. In so doing, 163 schools across Canada can benefit from donations, fund-raising events, and volunteers for school events.

The money fundraised by Wal-Mart from the public is matched "to a set amount" by Wal-Mart's Canadian head office. Given Wal-Mart's profit in 2000 of nearly $5.4 billion, contributions to 163 schools are a drop in the bucket.

"In recent market studies, Canadians have said that improving education at the elementary and secondary school levels in Canada is one of

Quick Facts:

▶ Cola Wars have in recent years spilled over into secondary schools. Maple Ridge school district was the first district in B.C. to sign an exclusive, secretive deal with Coke in December 1999. In the U.S., a school principal received a letter from a Coke official, urging that products be made available for purchase throughout the day, and that vending machines be placed in accessible spots to ensure the sales quota can be met.

▶ Terry Fox Secondary School in Port Coquitlam, B.C., became the first school in B.C. to contract with various fast-food companies in September 1999. Over 1,600 students and staff can now buy their junk food lunches in a food court that includes Subway, Pizza Hut, Great Canadian Bagel, and burgers and fries. Not only do fast food restaurants operating in school cafeterias sound the alarm one more time about the role of corporations in schools, but it also raises questions about the schools' commitment to good nutrition and health.

▶ The International Business Technology program at Gordon Graydon Memorial Secondary School in Mississauga trains students for work in various industries through partnerships with corporations, including Astra Pharma Inc., Bank of Nova Scotia, CIBC, Wood Gundy Securities Inc., Ontario Power Generation Inc., and Packard Bell NEC Inc. Corporate Partners offer equipment and sponsor events, as well as interview applicants, act as mentors to students and advisors to the program.

▶ ZapMe!, an American educational network, is as controversial as Channel One or its Canadian version, the Youth News Network. ZapMe! provides computer hardware and software to schools in the U.S. In exchange for the computers, schools promise to have students sitting in front of those computers for at least four hours every school day to ingest the advertising that constantly appears on the computer screen. Additionally, there have been reports that the software enables ZapMe! to track students' browsing habits as they surf.

their top 10 social concerns," said Dave Ferguson, President and CEO of Wal-Mart Canada. "Our Adopt-a-School Program makes it easy for our stores— our associates—to give back to their communities in a way that's meaningful to Canadians." (Wal-Mart has been regularly targeted with bad press for accusations of child labour, union-busting, and poor treatment of employees. The school "adoptions," however, are a public relations dream for projecting an image of good corporate citizenship, contributing to the community, and boosting customer loyalty.)

Resource Materials:

Barlow, Maude and Heather-jane Robertson, *Class Warfare: The Assault on Canada's Schools*, Key Porter, Toronto, 1994.

Kids for Sale: Taking a Stand Against Advertising in Our Schools. The Center for Commercial Free Public Education, California 1999.

Dunsmore, Diane. "Twelve Reasons to say 'No' to Corporate Partnerships." *CCPA Education Monitor*, Volume 4 Number 2, Spring 2000.

Maser, Michael. "Failing Kids with Fast Foods in the Cafeteria." *The Georgia Straight*, Vancouver, February 2000.

Robertson, Heather-jane. *No More Teachers, No More Books: The Commercialization of Canada's Schools.* McLelland & Stewart, Toronto, 1998.

Shaker, Erika. "Adopt a What?" *Our Times magazine*, Vol. 20, No. 2, April/May 2001.

Discussion Starters:

1. What kinds of business partnerships have been formed in schools within your community? What corporations are involved? What educational benefits do the schools and students get from these "partnerships"?

2. Do these "partnerships" involve training students for particular industries? Does this mean that schools become training grounds for corporations?

3 What is the effect of commercialization on the school and the students? Where should policy-makers, educators and families draw the line?

4. What, if any, kinds of policies or guidelines exist within the school or school board to manage commercialization and "partnerships"? What are some key demands or conditions that should be included in these guidelines?

2-c. Youth News Network

One of the more aggressive corporate manoeuvres to infiltrate the high school classroom today has been the Youth News Network (YNN). The YNN was incorporated in 1990, when its President, Rod MacDonald, began promoting a daily 12.5-minute "news" broadcast. The plan was to transmit a "news" program into participating Canadian classrooms, along with 2.5 minutes of commercials integrated throughout the broadcast. The concept of YNN is modelled after the American Channel One, which has access to 8.1 million students in the United States every day. In Canada, however, there was no guarantee of a buy-in from schools or advertisers, and so, initially, YNN quietly retreated.

But YNN resurfaced eight years later with bolder plans. Telescene Film Group, a Canadian entertainment company, had incorporated Athena Educational Partners, which relaunched YNN as a national distance education network. The news and current events broadcast would be aired during school time and high schools across the country would be linked to one another. In the fall of 2000, a merger between Athena and the Youth News Network with Sikaman Gold Resources Ltd. (SKG) was announced.

Through the advertisements, companies have direct access to a valuable market: namely, students. Given that students are required by law to attend school until the age of 16, schools are an advertiser's dream for reaching consumers. While Athena claims that students are not forced to view YNN, its contracts with school boards require that the daily program must be shown on at least 80% of the days that the school is open. Athena also reserves the right to request school attendance records to ensure advertisers are receiving a "return on investment."

In exchange for access to the captive audience, Athena Educational Partners offers schools an average of $150,000 worth of computer equipment, a television set for every classroom, a satellite dish, an internal distribution network, and a computer lab stocked with computers, a server, network hardware, a printer and software. The equipment is loaned to the school for the duration of the five-year contract; but if the contract is terminated after the six-month trial period, the equipment is removed.

The catch comes in the contract, which stipulates that Athena may use the equipment after school hours by renting it to private interests for educational purposes. This enables Athena to profit not only from the 12.5 minutes that YNN is broadcast in the classroom, but also from the use of school property itself.

The national launch of YNN was originally scheduled for the fall of 1999. However, lack of participation continually delayed the first broadcasts until January 2000. And even then, broadcasts being shown in just two schools fell far below the target of 50 schools that YNN had originally hoped to have participating. What's more, two schools would hardly comprise a national network, and no advertisers were on board.

While significant criticism has been raised in response to the advertising, there are other aspects of YNN that need to be addressed. YNN considers itself to be a current events program, but all of the current events commentary and analysis comes from one perspective: Athena's. Already, students and teachers have found that the broadcasts offer no deeper analysis of issues than students already know, and that the issues raised are not necessarily useful or reflective of curriculum.

An Educational Advisory Council, comprised of principals, teachers and students, was established to meet "regularly, and provide guidance for the daily broadcasts. How much input can they have when the council is spread across the country and broadcasts are daily?

Quick Facts:

▶ In 1999 Telescene estimated that 80% of revenue from YNN would be generated through sales of advertisements for the Youth News Network in high schools across the country.

▶ Athena announced in May, 1999, that as of September, "social advocacy" sponsored by corporations and governments will replace the 2.5 minutes of commercials.

▶ The Canadian Teachers' Federation's national survey from February 2000 showed that seven out of 10 Canadians are opposed to advertising of any kind in the classroom.

▶ Athena Educational Partners launched a lawsuit in May 2000 against People Against Commercial Television in Schools, a citizen organization opposed to biased news programs and commercials during class-time. Each individual named in the suit is being sued for $900,000.

▶ In July, 2000, the Peel District School Board voted to continue the partnership with YNN and to sign a new contract. Though no broadcasts have been shown since June 2000

Resistance/Activities:

The provincial governments in British Columbia, New Brunswick, Nova Scotia, P.E.I., Quebec, and the Yukon have banned YNN. But the resistance extends well beyond provincial governments.

"After listening to parents, teachers, school boards, and learning more about the proposal, it's time to turn the Youth News Network off in Nova Scotia. Every minute taken away from classroom time is an opportunity lost. You can't replace that time with your teacher with a television screen."—Wayne Gaudet, Education and Culture Minister, Nova Scotia. (InnovatioNS, April 1999.)

In Mississauga, the Peel School Board signed a five- year contract with YNN for Meadowvale Secondary School, despite opposition from students, teachers, and parents. Even before YNN was set up in the school, tensions were on the rise. In the spring of 1999, a student who had created an underground newspaper with an article about YNN was threatened with suspension, even though the paper had been developed and distributed off campus.

Students who opt out are treated with a different standard at Meadowvale. Students have had to obtain the signature of a parent or guardian (even if they are over 18 years old) and write an explanation of why they are opting out of viewing the broadcasts. Those who have opted out must spend that time in a separate room 'productively' and silently. In contrast, students do not have to have consent to view YNN during non-instructional time. YNN is now seen as an integral part of the school experience.

On May 25, 2000, a group of students from Meadowvale staged a walkout during the period in which YNN was regularly broadcast. Students sporting T-shirts with a circle and slash through YNN on the front and "Not for Sale" on the back distributed homemade cupcakes with anti-YNN logos in icing.

Discussion Starters:

1. What role does Athena/YNN play within schools in general, or in your school in particular? What are the implications of such arrangements? How is the agreement with Athena/YNN different than other business-school partnerships?

2. What risks are associated with advertising being integrated into newscasts? What are the implications of advertising being integrated into the official school time?

3. What effect does the presence of YNN have on the daily routine of the school day and on the school culture as a whole?

4. What sorts of actions could or have been taken to raise awareness about YNN in your school? What can be done to alert the wider community?

Resource Materials:

Brand, David. "Why YNN Sucks: Corporate Censorship in the Classroom." *Adbusters,* Aug./Sept. 2000.

Klein, Naomi. *No Logo.* Knopf Canada, Toronto, 2000.

Porter, Lindsay. "First In, First Out: A Crumbling Foothold for Commercial TV in Schools." *Adbusters,* Aug./Sept. 2000.

Robertson, Heather-jane. *No More Teachers, No More Books: The Commercialization of Classrooms.* McClelland & Stewart, Toronto, 1998.

Shaker, Erika. *Youth News Network and the Carpet-Bombing of the Classroom.* CCPA, Ottawa, 1999.

Shaker, Erika. *In the Corporate Interest: The YNN Experience in Canadian Schools.* CCPA, Ottawa, 2000.

2-d. Corporate Curriculum

Thinly disguised as educational resources and curriculum, corporations are taking commercialization to new levels. Many corporations, business associations, and think-tanks frame their propaganda in the form of curriculum—a term that implies a certain degree of knowledge, skills, and values.

By developing and distributing their own educational materials in the forms of books, kits, software, videos, and activity sheets, corporations demonstrate their blatant self-interest. Their profiles are raised, while they grant themselves access to sell their message and agenda, and instill their values in future workers. Corporate-sponsored materials often contain plugs for their products or company and can sometimes reflect biased opinions.

For instance, a Hostess potato chips' math supplement called "Count Your Chips" engaged students in a game of calculating how many chips the average person eats in a year, given the daily average. The game is played out in a framework with Hostess logos prominently displayed.

Environmental attacks in the form of educational resources have increased in recent years. Procter & Gamble espouses the virtues of clear-cutting in materials they produced: "Clear-cutting removes all trees within a stand of a few species to create new habitat for wildlife. P&G uses this economically and environmentally sound method because it most closely mimics nature's own process. Clear-cutting removes large tracts of timber, just as a forest fire would, except in a more controlled manner. Clear-cutting also opens the forest floor to sunshine, thus stimulating growth and providing food for animals."

Ontario Agri-Food Education, Inc., (OAFE) developed biotech educational resources. According to Ontario Agri-Food Technology Inc., the kits "will help to demystify" genetically engineered foods.

Banks and investment companies provide resources that talk about money management, savings and investments. A Royal Bank booklet on Banking and Money tells students how to open and use a bank account, how to write cheques and try new ways of banking. In the section on Saving and Spending your Money, students are told, "Everyone has goals. No matter who we are, there is something we all dream of being able to do that takes more money than we have now."

While cash-starved schools can find these materials helpful in the age of government cutbacks, schools run the risk of seeming to endorse particular products or the themes prominently displayed within them.

Business interests are given a helping hand by governments on all levels. For instance, the Ontario Ministry of Education and Training's new "rigorous" curriculum is designed to "ensure that students will be well prepared for their futures in the competitive, global economy. Changes to the curriculum, not only in Ontario, reinforce and legitimize this business mantra that has come to pervade the school environment.

Quick Facts:

▶ The McDonald's "Golden Arches" have become the most recognizable corporate image worldwide. McDonald's employs over 28,000 people globally—many of them teenagers. Their *"McEducator" Tool Kit*, introduced in the U.S., prepares students for employment while still in high school by offering resumé writing tips, sample cover letters, resumés, and tips for interviews and proper attire.

▶ Cisco Systems' Networking Academy Program has been offered through partnerships in over 130 Canadian schools for two years. Students at participating schools can enrol in the academy and are taught the Cisco curriculum by their teachers (who are trained by Cisco for 22 days.) Upon completion of the course, students can pay to take an examination and, if successful, become "Cisco Certified Networking Associates."

▶ Scholastic Inc. has developed a limited number of "sponsored" curriculum materials for corporations, including AT&T, McDonald's, and Chrysler.

▶ Johnson & Johnson, makers of OB tampons, offered physical education teachers who oversee health classes for girls aged 11 to 15—the OB target demographic— learning materials focused on self-esteem issues. The kit, with OB advertising on the cover and a message from the company inside, was sent to 3,000 schools across Canada.

▶ The Stock Market Game, made available by the Securities Industry Foundation for Economic Education, teaches students about economics and finance through a simulation of "how the world works." Students are given a hypothetical $100,000 worth of stocks to invest, and over 10 weeks they choose portfolios, follow the companies' performances, and make decisions about whether to buy, sell or trade.

Discussion Starters:

1. What experience have you had in your schools with curriculum programs provided by corporations? What corporations were sponsoring this material?

2. Describe the curriculum program or material provided by one of these corporations. What were some of the messages advocated by the sponsoring corporation?

3. What could be the long-term effects of a corporate-driven curriculum on teaching and freedom of speech in our schools? Who should control these corporate influences? Where should the line be drawn?

4. What actions could be taken to expose and challenge the specific cases of corporate-driven curriculum in our schools? What actions can be taken by students? By parents?

Resource Materials:

Kids for Sale: Taking a Stand Against Advertising in our Schools. The Center for Commercial-Free Public Education, California, 1998.

Robertson, Heather-jane. *No More Teachers, No More Books: The Commercialization of Classrooms.* McClelland & Stewart, Toronto, 1998.

Shaker, Erika. "Curriculum requirements different on 'Teen Planet.'" *CCPA Education Monitor*, June 1998.

Weinberg, Paul. "Public Schools, Private Dollars". *Eye Magazine*, March 9, 2000.

2-e. The Back to School Season

Market promotions signalling the end of the summer and the return to school have taken on a life of their own. By mid to late August it's almost impossible to step into a store of any variety and not be bombarded by the advertising gimmicks, luring young consumers and their parents to the till. The Back-to-School blitz is being transformed into a season of mass consumerism and a billion-dollar industry.

According to a report by YTV, the 2.5 million Canadian youth between 9 and 14 years of age have $1.8 billion in total discretionary income. Their influence over family purchases is ten times that amount. Statistics Canada estimated they influence an additional $18 billion worth of purchases. This summer, young consumers between ages 6 and 14 headed off to the mall with an average of $300 in their pockets to spend on back-to-school preparation—a total that has increased over the past few years.

Given these numbers, it's no surprise that corporations are tripping over themselves to tap into this market. But the prime reason for the great interest in young 'consumers' is not simply to ensure they are well prepared for school, but rather to cultivate and maintain loyalty to particular brands—and to the corporations themselves.

Corporations are teaming up to develop elaborate campaigns to draw young people to their stock of back-to-school essentials, including everything from clothes to school supplies to cellphones. For the past few summers, Grand and Toy teamed up with Much Music to target teens through their "Locker Search Event," a multi-week contest to win a locker stuffed with back-to-school supplies, a cellphone, a school concert, and cash. The 1999 campaign included television commercials aired on MuchMusic, with students searching in their lockers for a mock $5,000 cheque.

Marketing aimed at young people, specifically those identified as 'tweens'—aged 9-14—is not limited to the back-to-school season. Over the past few years, agencies and conferences are popping up all over to help marketers and advertisers tap into this lucrative market. Products and corporations are being avidly pitched to this powerful demographic. Even the stores where young people generally don't shop are being drawn in. Grocery stores, for instance, recognizing the influence teens have over household purchases, are tailoring their promotion to the 'needs' of the young, hedging their bets that the Moms who do the shopping will take notice.

Discussion Starters:

1. What are the different ways in which young people are targeted for marketing in your community and school?

2. How are you personally affected by advertising—by billboards, commercials, flyers, etc? What influences your choices and decisions?

3. What messages are young people sent about consumerism by the back-to-school blitz? What impact does this have on young people when they are directly targeted as consumers by marketeers peddling their products?

4. What can be done by youth to challenge the marketing techniques of the "back-to-school" blitz? What steps could be taken to confront business conferences designed to expand marketing techniques for young consumers?

Quick Facts:

▶ In 2000, tweens went to malls for back-to-school shopping with 17% more money than they had in 1999.

▶ Sherwood Park Mall in Alberta has, in the past, integrated an Activity Sign-Up as part of the back-to-school shopping season. Local organizations and clubs are invited to set up displays and information booths in the mall promoting their activities. Registering for extracurricular activities can be done as conveniently as shopping, and it's all under one roof. The event has been such a success that it has been repeated in March.

▶ In the late 1990s, at the Coquitlam Centre in B.C, a glossy back-to-school "Outta the pool, it's back to School" catalogue lured shoppers into the mall. Inside the catalogue, young consumers found contest forms to allow them to win $300. The contest was designed to boost a lucky student's back-to-school shopping budget.

Resource Materials:

Klein, Naomi. *No Logo*. Knopf Canada, Toronto, 2000.

"Back-to-School Powers Online Shopping Total: Spending on online sales increased from $4 billion in July to $4.2 billion in August." http://cyberatlas.internet.com/markets/retailing

PART II

EXPOSING
CORPORATE
RULE

WORK
&
COMMUNITY

3. IN COMMUNITIES

Powerful images have emerged from the mass demonstrations that have jolted the powers-that-be in Seattle, Washington, Prague, and Quebec City. Images of young people chanting "*Whose streets? Our streets*!" have focused attention on the conditions of our world in general, but, more specifically, on conditions in our communities. Globalization's impacts are felt most directly on the streets of communities, in the parks, in people's homes. It is here where agendas and policies are brought to life. It is also within these realms that the interconnectedness between economic globalization and communities tends to be overlooked.

Communities are places for people with shared interests to come together. But, all too often today, the interests of the community and society at large are usurped by the interests of development, economic integration, and big business.

Distinctive, culturally, socially and economically, diverse communities are being replaced with a sterilized, homogenized replica of a 'corporate' community. Rows of stores, restaurants, billboards and cars are interchangeable from community to community.

Our local identities are being lost, the commitment to creative, sustainable living on local levels supplanted by the 'convenience' of chain stores, fast food restaurants, and motor vehicles. Gentrification of communities pushes 'unwanted' residents out to make way for the 'wanted.' It creates illusions of safe, happy, crime-free communities. But it does nothing to resolve the fundamental problems that fester in many communities. The larger issues and concerns are simply pushed out of one neighbourhood into another one.

Globalization's impacts are felt differently in different communities—large and small, rural and urban—but they are felt in some way, nonetheless. The manifestations of globalization permeate every community. Small towns are increasingly becoming adjuncts of the larger cities as urban sprawl converts them into "bedroom" communities.

There is, of course, nothing new about this global urbanizing phenomenon and its impacts on community life. Yet, throughout the world, young people are sensing that these forces and trends are having a destructive effect on the quality of life on the planet. For these and related reasons, young people are starting to reclaim "community" in a variety of ways.

3-a. Private vs Public Space

Truly public space is fast disappearing. Concrete replaces grass, trees and gardens; openness gives way to fences; and once-spacious vistas are obstructed by billboards. Public space that has not been bought or branded by corporations is becoming scarce. Everywhere we turn, it seems as though we are being monitored by corporations, government, and security forces. The sense of community is under attack by corporate-induced isolation.

The struggle that has been waged against the privatization of health care, education, water systems, and other vital public services is now being waged in our physical environment. This form of privatization is turning our communities into concrete jungles. Distinctive community culture is being wiped out by the omnipresent outgrowths of economic globalization—cars, capital and consumerism.

The privatization of public spaces is leading to the physical reconstruction of our communities. Social interaction among citizens is now harnessed to corporate needs. Capital is brought back into the core, while people are relegated to the margins. Those already marginalized become virtual outcasts from a society that no longer wishes to help them or care for them.

Commercializing or privatizing public spaces is a lucrative business. Public washrooms, buses, garbage cans, billboards, even sidewalks have been conscripted by corporations eager to sell their messages anywhere. Virtually all public spaces are up for grabs.

And for young people, already targeted by marketers and advertisers for their 'deep pockets' and consumer habits, space untouched by corporations is at a premium. Parks, sidewalks, open spaces considered to be public are increasingly being patrolled, or worse still enclosed or levelled to make way for further industrial development. Places to be on your own or with friends, to think for yourself, are being swallowed up by ads urging us to buy the latest soft drink, junk food, or high-tech gadget.

Not only does privatizing public space grant access to corporations, but it also makes it easier to remove the people who once enjoyed and benefited from it. As concrete replaces green space, and as gentrification encroaches on established communities, the people who once utilized these attractive and restful spaces are pushed further away, out of sight.

But not far enough to escape the ceaseless tide of business ads. Take, for instance, the twist on billboards. They're large, and presumably get the corporate message across. But is it enough? Companies are now taking their advertisements to rolling billboards, such as those on trucks that rove through the city and environs, contributing to traffic congestion and air pollution. There seems to be no limit to the lengths to which corporations will go to batter our senses with their slogans and logos.

Quick Facts:

▶ In his book *Culture Jam*, Kalle Lasn states that "every day, an estimated 12 billion display ads, 3 million radio commercials, and more than 200,000 TV commercials" are aired.

▶ Trucks roaming through the streets with billboards are increasingly becoming a familiar sight in urban centres. Cash-strapped or entrepreneurial car owners can make money by having their cars converted into mobile commercials, as well as revealing detailed information about their lifestyles and driving habits. Global Positioning Systems are installed in the vehicle and, after the data is collected about the driver, the advertisement best suited to the targeted demographic group is painted on the vehicle. (www.autowraps.com)

▶ A City of Toronto proposal, ultimately rejected in 2001, would have seen a giant television billboard erected along the Bloor Street Viaduct over the Don Valley (including the pathway) as a means of funding a suicide barrier.

▶ A 1998 United Nations Development Report stated that global spending on advertising outpaces the growth of the world's economy by one-third. Total ad spending in the United States in 1998 reached $196.5 billion.

Resource Materials:

Adbusters, Vancouver, B.C., a monthly publication that specializes in the art of "culture jamming" by spoofing or satirizing corporate advertising.

Klein, Naomi. *No Logo*. Knopf Canada, Toronto, 2000.

Kressel, Shirley. "Privatizing the Public Realm." Available at http://csf.colorado.edu/mail/homeless/oct98/0020.html

Lasn, Kalle. *Culture Jam: How to Reverse America's Suicidal Consumer Binge - and Why We Must*. Quill, an Imprint of HarperCollins Publishers Inc., New York, 2000.

Discussion Starters:

1. In your travels today or this week, how many times have you witnessed an example of privatized or commercialized public space? What were some of the examples?

2. What are the impacts of privatizing public space in reducing accessibility to this space? What are the impacts in terms of gender, age, race, ethnicity, etc.? How are different people impacted?

3. What are the implications on the community itself, economically, culturally, physically, and socially? Why should young people be concerned about the privatization of public space?

4. What actions can be taken to expose and challenge the takeover of public space in our communities? What can be done to raise these issues in schools and on campuses? What can the Reclaim the Streets movement teach us about the kinds of action that can be taken?

Resistance/Activities:

"Reclaim the Streets" has become an annual party in many communities to take back public space that has been enclosed, isolated, or filled with concrete and cars. In May, 2000, in Toronto, hundreds of street partiers gathered in the financial district, Bay and King, to celebrate the 'reclaiming of the streets.' Music was played, dancing was enjoyed, and sod laid over the streets for all to enjoy.

On September 21, 2000, "Car-Free Day" turned urban centres around the world into car-free streets and opened space to pedestrians, bicycles, skateboards, rollerblades, wheelbarrows, wagons, push-scooters, and non-motorized vehicles.

In the past 10 years, cyclists in urban centres around the world have converged on the streets on a designated date every month to reclaim the streets. This critical mass winds its way through the streets, blocking other forms of traffic. Cyclists take the streets as a critical mass emphasizing alternatives to the primary mode of transportation—the automobile.

3-b. Disintegrating Neighbourhoods

The centrepiece of neighbourhoods is comprised of people. Rows of homes and buildings form the shape of the neighbourhood, but it is the children playing and the people gathering and interacting that bring it to life. It is the decisions that are made in the interests of the people that make a neighbourhood healthy and liveable.

As SUVs and minivans crowd the streets, and large big box developments pop up at ever-increasingly rates, a sense of community is weakened. The information age in which we live is touted as bringing people together, but how people come together is increasingly through technology—computer to computer, cell phone to cell phone—not in tangible interactions.

Isolation is carving itself into our neighbourhoods as people pile into cars and head out to the parameters of the city limits to the business parks and shopping complexes. Urban sprawl is transforming our cities and towns by eroding the cores of our neighbourhoods. It has brought American consumer culture into our neighbourhoods in little over a decade. Rows of strip malls and big box stores replace the small, locally-owned businesses in the downtown cores of many communities. Convenience is becoming the cornerstone of our neighbourhoods, along with an increasing reliance on cars and transnational chains.

Our neighbourhoods themselves are being redesigned for corporate convenience. We need only look around at the expansion of suburban developments, malls, and big box stores to see how our neighbourhoods are being redefined. The focus of bustling activity that used to occur within the downtown core of a community now occurs to a large degree at the city limits, with rows of industrial parks, strip malls, and big box complexes linked together by a maze of concrete and asphalt to facilitate the swift movement of cars from one mall to another.

The construction itself entails dependence on corporations. For everything from food to entertainment to cars, corporations are homogenizing our neighbourhoods. Fast food stores and grocery chains line the streets, pushing smaller, local businesses out. The streets are clogged with transnational chains that have no ties to the local neighbourhoods, but instead are outgrowths of the global economy that is changing and deforming local communities, isolating and segregating them.

Local connections are broken and once-distinctive neighbourhoods are being transformed into business parks and shopping centres devoid of community spirit and togetherness.

Beneath the overt symbols of globalization lies a more troublesome dilemma for our communities. The very identity and autonomy of communities is being usurped. Decision- making abilities are being shifted from the local to the international level, disempowering local government officials on decisions affecting everything from public services such as water, utilities and health to the by-laws set in place to determine the size and scope of development. For young people who have consistently had more difficulty accessing decision-makers and services, these transformations are pushing them into the streets.

It is the seemingly intangible aspects of globalization—the implications of international trade agreements, and the manoeuvring of transnational corporations—that pose the greatest threat to our neighbourhoods and the ways in which we live. Yet it puts McWorld into a much clearer context for youth.

Quick Facts:

▶ *For years the Disney Corporation has cultivated a fine mix of fantasy and magic through its theme-parks. Its "Worlds" and "Lands" have entrenched the "American way" and its values. In the mid-1990s, Disney took its development of theme-parks to a whole new level by designing Celebration, a small town in Florida that would bring the fantasy, magic, and old-fashioned values into the homes every day. The clustered neighbourhoods are built around the core of the community—Main Street shopping, a school, and health facilities. Celebration is the extension of the make-believe world Disney promotes. It has transported Disney's idyllic version of escapism to the bedrooms and kitchens of the middle class in this microcosm of old-fashioned America.*

▶ *Between 1990 and 1997, big box development in the Greater Toronto Area increased by more than 188%. There were more than 268 outlets taking up 11.1 million square feet of space.*

▶ *Urban sprawl/development uses five times more pipe and wire, five times as much heating and cooling energy than compact urban living. It costs us 35 times as much land and requires 15 times as much pavement.*

▶ *Between 1981 and 1986, prime agricultural land accounted for 59 per cent of all land in Canada converted to urban uses. Approximately 4,700 square kilometres of agricultural land (or one square kilometre daily) has been lost since 1981.*

Discussion Starters:

1. How has the face of your neighbourhood changed in your lifetime? Your parents' lifetime?

2. What are the implications of economic globalization and corporate rule on our neighbourhoods—ecologically, economically, culturally, and socially?

3. How does urban sprawl, development and technology impact your community, your neighbourhood?

Resource Materials:

Dobbin, Murray. "Who Will Tell Canada's Mayors? WTO Negotiations Threaten Municipal Government." *The Financial Post*, October 7, 2000.

Frantz, Douglas, and Collins, Catherine. *Celebration U.S.A.: Living in Disney's Brave New Town*. Henry Holt and Company, 1999.

Jones, Kenneth G. and Michael J. Doucet. *The Big Box, The Big Screen The Flagship and Beyond: Impacts and Trends in the Greater Toronto Area.* Centre for the Study of Commercial Activity, July 1998.

3-c. Women's Rights

Young women of today's generation have grown up in the wake of the victories for women's rights fought by their grandmothers, mothers, friends and mentors. The world in which we live is dramatically different from the world in which our mothers and grandmothers lived. But the rights we have and the rights we continue to fight for are not guaranteed, and so the struggle for equality continues and takes on different forms in the light of globalization.

The impacts of economic globalization felt by women are not gender neutral. Women comprise more than half of the world's population. They perform nearly two-thirds of the world's work hours, receive one-tenth the world's income, and own less than one-hundredth of the world's property. The inequalities still felt by women are profound.

Women have throughout history played vital roles in building, sustaining, and strengthening communities. This remains true today, as evidenced by their unpaid work in the home, as well as their role outside the home: nurturing communities and helping to build them. As globalization's impacts are localized, it is women who are most affected. The responsibilities of family and home remain,
but the responsibilities of the larger community increase: doing the work that used to be done by social programs, responding to the toll globalization is taking, and keeping communities together.

The inequalities are exacerbated by the deregulation of markets, the liberalization of trade, the massive restructuring of work, and the privatization of services and social programs. While the results of economic globalization—increased poverty, reduced access to services, and growing inequalities—claim many victims, the burden of alleviating the ill-effects falls mainly upon women.

As globalization's effects are more deeply entrenched, the gains women have fought for over the generations are undermined. For women, no experts are needed to explain the role corporations and globalization play in their lives. The painful impacts are felt every day in homes, communities, at work (both paid and unpaid), and through discrimination and oppression. These effects of the global economy are felt to varying degrees by nearly all women, but especially by women of colour and Aboriginal women, who are most adversely affected.

Markets have historically tried to control, define and undervalue women's identities and participation in the home, in public spheres, and in workplaces. The ideological shift embodied in economic globalization further undermines and undervalues women's roles in society. Governments now make decisions and policies in the interests of business, in the name of greater competitiveness and freer trade. Our political system now puts corporations and their perceived rights before the rights of people and communities.

Corporations themselves buy our public services, increasing the burden of unpaid work on women, forcing them to pick up the slack as services become less accessible and affordable.

The extra burdens placed on women are by no means solely economic. The unpaid contributions of women to homes, communities and workplaces are invisible and unrecognized in this system that values business activity and markets. For women, the wage gap and the unequal distribution of wealth continue to grow. Women still earn less than men—only 73% of what men earn for a full year. Changes to unemployment insurance have especially hurt women, who comprise approximately 70% of part-time workers.

Cutbacks to health care, education, and social services, as well as the lack of adequate child-care, have put increased responsibilities on women, adding to the pressure that already existed in terms of the onerous unpaid work that women are expected to perform.

Quick Facts:

▶ More than 81% of Canada's single mothers with children under the age of seven are living in poverty.

▶ In a single generation, the percentage of young families living in poverty has more than doubled: from 22% to 46%. In 1989, households represented by the top fifth of income earners received $18 for every dollar earned by those in the bottom fifth. By 1998, the gap had widened to $27 to $1. (Anne Golden)

▶ In 1980, 334 neighbourhoods in Canada were considered poor, with a poverty rate double the national average. Nearly 12% of all families with incomes below StatsCan's unofficial poverty line lived in these areas. Fifteen years later, the number of poverty-ridden neighbourhoods had jumped to 567, while the proportion of poor Canadian families residing in them rose to 18%.

▶ Child poverty in Canada increased by 60% during the decade of the 1990s. According to a report released by the City of Toronto in January 2000, 50,000 children depend on food banks for their meals each month in Toronto, along with 60,000 adults.

Discussion Starters:

1. In what ways are you, your mothers, sisters, and friends impacted on a daily basis by economic globalization? Give some examples.

2. Can you connect the dots between the impacts you feel and live locally and the broader context? How do these impacts affect women in different regions of Canada and the world?

3. What happens to the quality of community life when women become targets of economic globalization?

4. What action could be taken by young people today to preserve and expand women's rights in the age of corporate globalization? What action have you taken already? What tools and support do women need to participate in resistance and working toward change?

Resistance/Activities:

Throughout 2000, women from every corner of the world drew attention to the increased poverty and continued violence faced by women. Discussions, workshops, rallies and demonstrations addressed these issues under the banner of the World March of Women. In Canada, eight months of activity culminated on October 15 with 50,000 women, children and men on Parliament Hill demanding an end to poverty and to violence against women. Internationally, the months of campaigning and demonstrating culminated in the streets of New York City outside and inside the United Nations on October 17.

Resource Materials:

Barndt, Deborah. *Women Working the NAFTA Food Chain*. Second Story Press. Toronto. 1999.

Griffin Cohen, Marjorie, Laurell Ritchie, Michele Swenarchuk and Leah Vosko. *Globalization: Some Implications and Strategies for Women.* The National Action Committee on the Status of Women (Canada), June 1998.

"World March of Women 2000 Mobilizing/Organizing Workshops." Ontario Federation of Labour and the Ontario Coalition for Social Justice, March 21- April 19, 2000.

Townson, Monica. "The Feminization of Poverty: Women in Canada remain among "poorest of the poor." *CCPA Monitor*. Volume 7, No. 1. May 2000.

3-d. Migration/Immigration

Globalization has also opened national borders to a greater flow of goods and services. As the barriers come down, the process of migration has accelerated, with significant repercussions on both the communities that people leave and those to which they migrate.

While the effects of forcing people to migrate remain diverse, the causes of migration are driven by political and economic forces. Within the context of the global economy, it is the market that forces people to migrate in search of work, to sell their skills and labour. Worldwide, 80 million people unable to earn a living in rural areas have been forced to move to the cities. Environmental degradation, including desertification, unsustainable development and economic expansion, force millions of millions of people to relocate.

The face of Canada has changed dramatically in past decades. Approximately one-third of the estimated 200,000 immigrants who come here each year are young people under the age of 25. By 2005, half of the Canadian population will be people of colour. Toronto and Vancouver are already among the 10 most ethnically diverse cities in the world. In spite of the diversity, few gains have been secured for people of colour, and

the darker a person's skin, the more devastating the impacts. Systemic racism and inequalities are perpetuated.

Migrants to Canada have historically been an economic tool for big business' development projects. Canadian immigration policy has always twinned racism and economic discrimination. Policies themselves reflect the economic times. Influxes of immigration occur during periods of economic activity and prosperity, decreases during periods of recession. The treatment of immigrants has also reflected the values of the work they are made to do. Chinese migrants in the 19th century, for example, built the transcontinental railroads, and were exploited, underpaid, and forced to pay exorbitant head taxes.

Tens of millions of people flow in and out of Canada every year. Professionals from Canada's NAFTA and WTO partners are welcomed with open arms, but during the summer of 1999, when Chinese migrants arrived on the shores of B.C., they were told to go home.

Transnational corporations have driven down the costs of doing business, and international trade structures have opened borders—all of which enables corporations to shift their operations to where labour is cheapest and taxes are lowest. In the age of globalization, freedom of movement for goods and services are guaranteed, but human rights and the freedom of mobility for workers are excluded.

Workers are becoming an exportable commodity, forced to follow the trail of jobs from community to community, country to country. Worldwide, one in 100 people now live outside their country of birth, and 30 million people have been forced to relocate within their own countries as a result of industrial projects that has destroyed their livelihood.

The young people who have immigrated here bring with them the experiences of their homes. Young people of colour born here carry the experience of living with the hostility of racism and injustice, as well as with the impacts of globalization on their daily lives.

Given the ever-increasing diversification of our communities, misconceptions and xenophobia persist. Majority world countries have a responsibility to protect people from forced migration. If people were not forced to make decisions dislocating their lives based on the need to earn a living or simply to survive, migration could be voluntary—but the global economy forces millions of people to uproot their lives and leave their homes.

Quick Facts:

▶ Over 35 million people work overseas. Asian women are the fastest growing category of foreign workers.

▶ Ten million people worldwide have left their homes because they cannot make a living from the land. By the end of the 1990s, approximately 60 million people were made landless/homeless by environmental degradation.

▶ The City of Toronto has Canada's largest immigrant population. More than 50% of the city's population are immigrants and refugees. Over 70,000 immigrants come to Toronto each year.

▶ In 1998, the U.S. spent $495 million on the incarceration of illegal migrants.

Discussion Starters:

1. What impact has globalization and economic policy had on immigration, refugees, and other domestic policies that affect communities of colour?

2. How do social, economic and political policies affect communities differently?

3. What does it say about the face of Canada in the future when people of colour will make up more than half our population by 2025?

4. What work needs to be done on local and national levels to address the inequities in policies and the way they adversely affect people? What kind of leadership could be taken by today's youth?

Resource Materials:

Ride, Anouk. "Maps, Myths and Migration." *The New Internationalist*, Issue 305, September 1998.

Sivanadan, Ambalavaner. "Casualties of Globalism." *The Guardian*. August, 2000.

3-e. A Virtual Police State

Young people have been targets of policy-makers for years. Policies have stereotyped young people as lazy and irresponsible, as prone to criminal behaviour, and thus in need of close monitoring, constraints and punishment. During this period of laissez-faire capitalism, being poor—and especially being both young and poor—is not acceptable.

Police forces have always been used to protect the interests of the rich and powerful. The end of the cold war turned the international security forces inwards to become the enforcers of domestic "law and order" policies. Crime rates have steadily decreased, yet the rate of incarceration goes up and police forces continually lobby for increases in their budgets.

Governments on every level are implementing social and economic policies that punish the most vulnerable in our society. Federal transfer payments to the provinces, welfare, social assistance, and unemployment insurance have all been cut. Changes to the Young Offenders' Act and other pieces of legislation crack down on panhandling and loitering, targeting particular neighbourhoods and people on the streets in general. Rather than addressing the social inequities that are ravaging our communities and taking corrective action, governments opt to hire and train more police and empower them to harass, intimidate and imprison the most vulnerable members of society.

The big criminals go unchecked. They find crime to be profitable. Corporations commit crimes every day in their ruthless pursuit of profit, but are left untouched by the authorities. It is their victims—those who have been most grievously hurt by profit-driven corporations—who are targeted and labelled as criminals, or as the people most likely to engage in criminal behaviour.

The privatization of policing services reduces accountability to the public. Information about private prisons becomes difficult to obtain, since they are not subject to the same regulations as provincial agencies. Private corporations involved in the privatization of prisons have a poor track record in the U.S., England and Australia—not to mention that the rates of incarceration in those countries are among the highest worldwide. The increased presence of police and private security forces in communities is not only limited to "cleaning up" or "increasing the quality of life," but also protecting capital and the political and business élite. Criminal behaviour is being redefined to preserve the flow of capital. Our civil liberties and our rights are stripped away in the attempt to shield the rich and powerful from demonstrations of public dissent.

The world was stunned by the force used by police in Seattle, Quebec City and Genoa, and the transformation of those cities into virtual police states to protect the corporate and political pushers of free trade. Rows of

Quick Facts:

▶ *Community Action Policing, a $1.9 million program, was introduced in Toronto in the summer of 1999 and brought back again in 2000 to focus on "problem areas" in response to concerns about "community safety and tourism," as well as to secure additional funds to pay officers overtime. Under the program, people have reported to an independent committee that they have been physically threatened and beaten, their photographs have been taken without consent, they have been ticketed, searched without cause, arrested on false or improper charges, and have had possessions confiscated that in some cases have been destroyed or not returned.*

▶ *According to Statistics Canada, the overall crime rate in 1999 declined to the lowest level in 20 years, falling for the eighth consecutive year. Youth crime dropped 7.2% in 1999—21% lower than it was 10 years ago. But the Canadian rate of youth incarceration is twice that of the United States, and 10 to 15 times higher than the rate per 1,000 youth in many European countries, Australia and New Zealand.*

▶ *New Brunswick contracted out prison management to Wackenhut Corporation in 1995. Wackenhut compiled three million dossiers on "potential American subversives" during the 1960s; the files were eventually handed over to the FBI.*

▶ *The Ontario government has announced plans to privatize some of its prisons. The plans include management of new "super-jails," running new boot camps, and providing inmate services, such as food and work programs.*

▶ *Over three days in Quebec City during the summit of the Americas, 4,709 canisters of tear gas and 822 plastic bullets were fired at protesters. Some 6,700 police officers and 1,500 soldiers were assigned to protect government leaders and corporate executives. The security costs of the Summit exceeded $1 million.*

▶ *During the protests against the WTO in Seattle, the Pentagon's top-secret Delta Force, which was prominent in the WACO standoff, established its own command post in a downtown hotel.*

▶ *In a Rand study prepared for the Pentagon, civil society activists against corporate globalization are portrayed as an "NGO swarm" that can "sting a victim to death" through the Internet. The Pentagon has reportedly begun "social net wars" to stir up conflict among civil society groups over controversial issues.*

▶ *The United States—land of the free—is home to 5% of the world's population, yet it accounts for 25% of the world's prisoners. The American prison industry is the second largest employer in the U.S. after General Motors.*

police in riot gear used tear gas, rubber bullets and water cannons to quell peaceful protesters, including many thousands of young people, brutally depriving them of their democratic right to protest. The images of those heavily armoured and armed police—and especially the concrete and chain-link fence in Quebec City, the obscene attacks on people in Genoa—were televised all around the world, to cities in other countries where similar protests against corporate globalization have occurred, or will occur in future.

Our domestic rights to protest, to assemble, and to speak freely are increasingly being stripped away. Those who oppose or criticize economic and social injustice, or who challenge the powers-that-be, are being criminalized. A Canadian Secret Intelligence Service (CSIS) report released in 2000 describes "militant anarchists" as the opponents of capitalism. In the lead-up to large-scale mobilizations

Resistance/Activities:

Resistance to the international security boom has taken a variety of forms, with groups employing different strategies to approach the different components of the threat. Right across the country, in a variety of communities, activists have been organizing against the attacks on the poor and the criminalization of the poor.

University and college students across North America have forced Sodexho Marriott Services, one of North America's largest food service providers on campuses, to take notice that student fees for food will not be used to support Sodexho Marriott's parent company, Sodexho Alliance, or its investments in the Corrections Corporation of America, the largest private prison company. On campuses across North America, students have begun actively organizing, raising awareness, and making the links. Students at State U of N.Y. at Albany, Evergreen State College, Goucher College, and James Madison University in the U.S. have been successful in getting Sodexho Marriott off their campuses. In December 2000, a series of student groups engaged in occupations on their campuses to send a message that they will not be used, nor will their money be used, as part of the private prison industry. In June 2001, Sodexho Alliance announced it would sell its stock in the Corrections Corporation of America.

The actions of police and the suppression of dissent during and following the summit of the Americas in Quebec City have led over 100 organizations and individuals to call for an inquiry into the actions and methods used by the government and government agencies to suppress freedom of speech and assembly. The social and environmental impacts of the police actions and the consequences for the future of democracy in Canada were also cited as legitimate issues for such an inquiry.

and even in community-based organizing on local issues, individuals and groups are targeted, routinely surveyed, harassed, and even arrested. On the streets of Quebec City, protesters were "snatched" off the streets and arrested, simply for carrying gas-masks or medical supplies. In Genoa, a midnight raid of a school woke sleeping protesters with terrifying force.

Clearly, governments that serve only the corporations—including those in Canada and other supposedly democratic countries—now openly condone the suppression of the basic freedoms of speech and assembly by the unrestrained use of police clubs, tear gas, pepper spray, water cannons, and arbitrary arrest and imprisonment.

Discussion Starters:

1. How has the role of "maintaining security" or policing changed in your community? What have you heard about or experienced with respect to this agenda and its enforcement in communities?

2. How does the emphasis on crime, security and policing impact your community, the sense of safety, services and programs? Does it affect the priorities for developing strong, healthy communities?

3. What are the implications of this agenda, particularly the issue of targeting, on issues such as gender, race, ethnicity, sexual orientation, political association? What examples do you know of that reflect the impacts of targeting particular individuals or groups of people based on the issues identified?

4. What strategies and tactics have been used or could be used to ensure that civil and human rights are not violated, to ensure safety, and to address the broader context of security issues?

Resource Materials:

Who's the Target? An Evaluation of Community Action Policing. Committee to Stop Targeted Policing. Toronto, August 2000.

Gerlach, Loretta. "The Rise of the Police State: Why the WTO, World Bank and the IMF have to turn cities into virtual police states in order to hold their meetings". *Briarpatch Magazine*, June 2000.

Parenti, Christian. *Lockdown in America: Police and Prisons in the Age of Crisis.* Verso, New York, 1999.

Parenti, Christian. "The Prison Industrial Complex: Crisis and Control." *Corporate Watch*, September 1999.

Schlosser, Eric. "The Prison-Industrial Complex." *Atlantic Magazine*, December 1998.

Stewart, Lyle. "Getting Spooked." *THIS Magazine.* Vol. 34, No. 5. March/April 2001.

4. IN THE WORKPLACE

For all the talk about the growth of the economy and job creation over the past few years, unemployment is still crippling communities. Workplaces are being dramatically transformed. The very nature of work itself is being redefined. Young workers face uncertain prospects. Youth unemployment exceeded 20% in 1997—the highest point during the 1990s. Youth participation in the labour market was at its lowest in 25 years. The uncertainties faced by young people are not because they lack knowledge or skills; in fact, they are the highest educated generation in Canadian history. The problems they face stem primarily from economic corporate globalization and the policies that support it.

Youth employment has always been dependent on the business cycle. As unemployment rises, young workers are squeezed out of the workforce, but during economic expansion their workplace participation increases. While there has been a burst of high-tech, high-skilled jobs in the past 10 years, low-skilled jobs have declined. Youth employment has dropped partly because of the lack of jobs, but also because of the desire of more young people to stay in school longer.

For those with jobs, instability and insecurity pervade their working conditions to a large extent. While free trade and globalization have opened borders, government policies have weakened and in some cases dismantled workers' protections, leading to a decline in wage rates and in the quality of work itself. Technology has changed methods of production. Operations and management have been reorganized. And most new jobs take the form of temporary, casual and part-time employment, which is in most cases insecure and poorly paid. The past decade has been one of keeping profits up and labour costs down.

These changes in the labour market profoundly affect today's young people, making them worse off than previous generations. Overall employment rates have increased since the early 1990s, but in 1997 youth participation in the labour force was at its lowest point in 25 years. In Ontario, the rate of participation has dropped by almost 10% since 1989. In the early 1990s, young workers were earning 30% less in real terms than in the early 1980s. And increasingly, young people are working at multiple jobs to pay for food, and other essentials like rent—not to mention their student loans.

Changes to the nature of work have been accompanied by a nationwide weakening of the legislation that protects workers, stripping away their rights and leaving them (particularly the younger ones) vulnerable to abuses of power by employers. In the fall of 2000, for example, the Ontario government passed sweeping changes to the Employment Standards Act, extending the work week from 40 hours to 60, and enabling employers to force workers to take their two week holidays a few days at a time.

The summer jobs in retail or the service sector—jobs that provide students with little more than pocket change—are no longer a stepping stone along the career path to the "dream job" in McWorld. They are quickly becoming dead-end careers. And as this shift continues, young people equipped with degrees are compelled to stay longer in those low-paid positions, making it even more difficult for high school students and other young people to find jobs, even for the summer.

4-a. Contingent Workers

The nature of work has steadily shifted in the last 30 years towards more precarious forms of employment. Throughout the 1990s, workplaces have been transformed to reflect the business mantra of competitiveness and flexibility, and the concurrent changes in government policy made to accommodate the corporate agenda. In the process, workers have been transformed into an expendable, insecure, just-in-time army. Temporary employment has always existed, but it is now much more prevalent and has spread into almost all sectors *of the economy. Temp agencies are now the largest employers in North America.*

The "flexibility" of this form of work is promoted as liberating, providing more time for leisure activities, and granting workers more control over their jobs. We are told that we can do anything we want, that we don't need to define ourselves as workers, but rather as self-employed contractors or "consultants." But the reality is job insecurity and instability, and no benefits. The casualization of work continues to entrench and define jobs based on gender, race, and ethnicity. The traditional roles and responsibilities of governments and employers are reduced or eliminated, leaving workers on their own in a swamp of insecurity and "contingency."

Contingent work refers not only to the temporary aspect of work and jobs. It also gives employers greater flexibility in hiring and setting work schedules based on the requirements of production, supply and demand. In many industries, benefits associated with permanent employment have been reduced or even eliminated for contingent workers, including pensions, drug and dental plans, and even overtime and vacation pay.

The impacts of this transformation from permanent work to more precarious forms of employment hit women, immigrants, and young workers particularly hard. The "liberation" of flexible work means juggling multiple jobs or contracts to make ends meet, while coping with the responsibilities of family and school.

At any given time, there can be thousands of individuals employed by a temp agency, but only a small percentage of them may be working. There is no guarantee

Discussion Starters:

1. Do you and your friends have jobs? What kind of jobs do you hold? Permanent, part-time, casual, seasonal, etc? What sorts of wages, benefits, and working conditions do you have?

2. What are the implications of contingent or precarious work on young people? Women? Immigrants? Workers of colour? Why are these workers more adversely affected, and how?

3. What are the responsibilities of employers and government to ensure that workers' rights are protected? Are these responsibilities being met by employers and government? If not, what should be done to put pressure on them to live up to their responsibilities?

4. What can be done in your community, school or campus to raise public awareness about these issues?

of work from day to day, since contingent workers' schedules are set by the employers according to the amount of work they need to have done at any given time. The inconsistency of work and contracts exposes contingent workers to high levels of stress and anxiety.

Young people are urged by the mainstream corporate media to be well-trained and competitive workers. They are told about the skills they should acquire to be successful in the global economy—but at the same time they are being warned not to expect to obtain full-time permanent jobs. The contradiction in messages is stark. Young people are urged to "take control" of their futures, while their futures are being undermined. For young people, it adds up to the reality that work now exists within a culture of insecurity.

Quick Facts:

▶ One in five non-union workers are in part-time jobs, compared to one in eight union members.

▶ Milwaukee-based employment agency Manpower Inc. , is among the largest employers in the U.S., employing over 2.1 million workers worldwide.

▶ Half of all young people and one-quarter of adult women work part-time hours, compared with one in 20 adult men in Canada.

▶ Between May 1998 and May 1999, one in four new jobs created were temporary.

Resource Materials:

Youth At Work in Canada: A Research Report. Canadian Council on Social development. Ottawa, 1998.

DeWolff, Alice. "The Face of Globalization: Women Working Poor in Canada." *Women 2000: Eradicating Poverty and Violence in the 21st Century. Canadian Woman Studies,* Volume 20, Number 3, University of Toronto Press, Toronto, 2000.

Jackson, Andrew, David Robinson, Bob Baldwin and Cindy Wiggins. *Falling Behind: The State of Working Canada, 2000*. Canadian Centre for Policy Alternatives, Ottawa, 2000.

Laxer, Kate. "Youth Roll-Call." *Our Times Magazine,* Youth Conference Issue, Volume 18, Number 1, January, February 1999.

Scott, Rob, in Carlos, Salas & Bruce Campbell. *NAFTA at Seven: Impact on Workers in All Three Nations.* Economic Policy Institute, Washington DC. April 2001.

Spink, Lynn. "Living on the Edge: The Not-So-Casual World of Contingent Workers." *Our Times Magazine*, Volume 19, Number 3, July/August 2000.

Vosko, Leah. *Temporary Work: The Gendered Rise of a Precarious Employment Relationship*. University of Toronto Press, Toronto, 2000.

4-b. Retail

When young people start looking for jobs these days, they are far more likely to wind up as a low-wage, non-unionized service employee than as a reasonably well- paid, unionized worker. Retail, fast food, and other service industries are where the majority of young workers end up. Their workplaces are usually small, with fewer than 20 employees. The service industry is among the lowest paying in Canada.

Shops, storefronts and malls are the most obvious sign of the retail sector. The clothing industry employs 100,000 Canadian workers at more than 2,000 establishments, plus 56,000 in the textile industry. These industries produce about $15 billion worth of goods for the Canadian market, and for exports. It is Canada's eighth largest provider of manufacturing jobs. For many young workers, the part-time job in retail has become a career. Tired of low wages, erratic shifts, onerous rules to follow while on the job, young people are looking for ways to improve their working conditions. Many are attempting to unionize their workplaces as a way to bring needed change.

While the workplaces themselves are small, the employers are generally large, many of them transnational and highly profitable. Wal-Mart had sales of $165 billion for the 2000 fiscal year, an increase of 20%. They employ more than 1.14 million "associates" worldwide. In 1996, Wal-Mart's revenues exceeded the GDP of 161 countries, including Poland and Israel. Another example is the Gap, which generated $11.6 billion in revenue from its 3,018 stores worldwide in 1999. Chapters bookstores constitute a quarter of the Canadian retail book market. They generated $577.9 million in revenues in 1999, and employ over 6,000 workers across Canada, many of them young people.

Despite what they may claim, these transnational corporations that employ thousands of Canadian young people are not hard pressed for cash. They make huge profits by paying the workers who sew our clothes and the workers who sell them low wages, in many cases not even a living wage. When the B.C. government announced its intention to increase the minimum wage in that province last year, the Retail Council of Canada, an association of over 8,500 department, speciality, discount and independent stores, was outraged. In a survey conducted by the Council, most stores said they would offset the minimum wage increase by reducing the hours of employees or laying some of them off.

This profit-obsessed corporate mentality permeates the retail stores. "Teamwork" and "smiles" help to create an environment that brings customers through the doors. Stores are staffed by "associates," "partners," and "sales consultants" who generally earn the bare minimum wage, or slightly more, for part-time or casual work.

Before the products are placed on the shelves, they have to be made by millions of workers around the world, many of them children, most of whom are exploited, ill-treated, and extremely low-paid. But not all sweatshop workers are in the Third World. There are hundreds of sweatshops right in our own backyard. Most clothing made in Canada, for example, is also produced by workers—generally female immigrants—who are paid the minimum wage or less. A study of homeworkers in the Greater Toronto Area showed that the average wage of homeworkers is $5-6 an hour. Some are paid as little as $2 an hour.

Quick Facts:

▶ *Statistics Canada reported in August 2000 that the average weekly earnings of employees in the retail sector amounted to $374.70. That's $1,498.80 for the month. Based on that rate of pay sustained over the year, they would earn $17,985.60.*

▶ *In May 2000, almost half of the 891,000 young workers in Ontario worked in sales and services.*

▶ *Wal-mart founder Sam Walton came up with the idea of the Wal-Mart "cheer" while visiting a factory in Korea. It is supposed to let the workers have fun and subsequently work better.*

▶ *There are an estimated 40,000 homeworkers in Canada's garment industry, as many as 8,000 in Toronto. The majority of homeworkers are not eligible for statutory holiday pay or vacation pay, or to unemployment insurance when out of work or between jobs. Their employers do not usually make contributions to EI or the Canada Pension Plan. Many homeworkers forced to work long hours suffer from back or shoulder pain.*

Resistance/Activities

In 1997, workers at Wal-Mart in Windsor, Ontario, became the first employees at a Wal-Mart store anywhere in the world to join a union. The workers were particularly outraged by Wal-Mart's degrading policy of having workers engage in the Wal-Mart cheer and callisthenics every morning. Wal-Mart was able to drag out contract negotiations and eventually persuaded the workers to vote for the union's decertification, but nevertheless the initial move to unionize has led to other workers following their lead and launching organizing drives at other Wal-Mart stores.

Part-time workers at the University of Toronto bookstore walked the picket line for 12 weeks last year to fight for a fair contract, including better wages and recognition of the union.

Discussion Starters:

1. As a young worker or someone who will one day be working, what are your basic rights? Do you know where to find the information that outlines your rights?

2. What are the major retail food employers in your community or region? How many jobs do they create? What are the starting wages? What are the working conditions like? Are the jobs temporary, part-time, or full-time?

3. What role do unions play for workers? Why would being a union member be advantageous? If you're working in retail, is your job organized? Have you ever contemplated approaching a union? What issues would arise in the workplace if you did approach a union?

4. What steps have been taken in your workplace, or community, to raise awareness about working conditions and rights? What is the role of the employer and the role of the government in enforcing laws and regulations to ensure that workers' rights are respected? What improvements could lead to better working conditions in the retail sector?

Resource Materials:

Livesey, Bruce. "McJob Hell. Young workers contend with low pay, lousy hours and creepy bosses." *Eye Magazine*, Toronto, June 24, 1999.

Homeworkers in Canada. Maquila Solidarity Network, May 2000.

Sayles, Susan. "For Employees Only: A Short Story from the Other Side of the Door." *Our Times Magazine.* Dec. 1999/Jan. 2000.

4-c. Fast Food

The fast food industry is one of the largest employers of young people. More than half of the young workers in this sector are now over 25 years old. Food service corporations are highly profitable in this age of eating on the go. And they are setting up shop virtually everywhere. There are over 26,000 McDonald's restaurants in 119 countries. Starbucks has over 22,000 outlets worldwide.

Transnational food service corporations have left their mark on the global stage. They have exported their culture, image, and menus across regional borders. Serving customers in all corners of the world has been made interchangeable from one restaurant to another.

Fast food chains and coffee outlets are dependent on their workers. They project ideal working environments, team-work, and special training to prepare them for their futures in the food industry. McDonald's claims to 'be the best employer for [their] people in each community around the world." Starbucks' "Special Blend" pay program is "unique to the employees and what [they] do at Starbucks." The reality for most workers, however, is quite the opposite.

Young workers' stories about their working conditions in the fast food industry have been told and retold for years. Countless articles have been written and websites constructed, all devoted to frustrating work experiences. The majority of outlets hire young people to work, part-time or casually, for low wages in poor working conditions, and often subjected to verbal harassment by managers.

In the past, many of these workers found it easier to quit the job and move on to another one when the conditions became unbearable. But as the number of young people seeking jobs increases while high unemployment and underemployment persist, they are increasingly staying in these "mcjobs" longer. And many are now turning to unions for support.

High staff turnovers in services, and the part-time and casual nature of the work, makes the sector difficult for traditional organizing drives. But there have been successes, in spite of rabidly anti-union sentiments among many corporations, most notably McDonald's.

Working conditions are generally bad enough, but when workers approach unions, those conditions are invariably worsened by irate managers. Young workers have reported arbitrary reductions in hours, intimidation by management, visits from managers at their homes—even being fired after they've initiated a union organizing campaign.

For those who are successful, what lies ahead is often just as difficult. Very few attempts to organize McDonald's restaurants have been successful. In 1993, Sara Inglis, at the time a high school student, tried to organize the McDonald's she worked at in Orangeville, Ont., but the attempt was squashed. In 1998, workers at a McDonald's in St. Hubert, Que., successfully organized their workplace with the Teamsters, only to see management shut the franchise down two weeks later, citing financial bankruptcy. Later in 1998, Tessa Lowinger and Jennifer Wiebe, two high school students in Squamish, B.C., decided they wanted to join a union to fight for better working conditions, and were ultimately successful in winning the right to have the Canadian Auto Workers represent them. The workers were induced to have the union decertified a year later, but it remains the first McDonald's restaurant to be unionized in North America.

Persistence on the part of workers and unions have brought significant gains. Workers fighting for greater power in their workplace, better working conditions and fairer wages, make significant gains not only for themselves, but for other workers as well.

Quick Facts:

▶ *Statistics Canada reported in August 2000 that the average weekly earnings of employees in accommodation, food and beverage services were $242.65 in June. That's $970.60 for their labours that month. Based on that rate of pay sustained over the year, they would earn $11,647.20— an amount that falls below the poverty line.*

▶ *According to the Job Search Canada website, teenagers face the dilemma of little or no work experience when looking for a job. The Canadian Council on Social Development's 1998 report on Youth and Work showed that 58% of 16-year-olds had never held a job in 1998, compared to 26% in 1989.*

▶ *The big business magazine Fortune named Starbucks one of "The 100 Best Companies to Work For" in 1997 and 1998. In 1999, a new Starbucks opened every 16 hours.*

▶ *The Report on Business Magazine in February 2000 ranked McDonald's Restaurants of Canada the fourth best company to work for. Perks that were cited include profit-sharing for full-time employees and an eight- week paid sabbatical after 10 years for salaried employees.*

Resistance/Activities:

Workers at Starbucks' 12 unionized outlets went on "unstrike" in October 1999. The workers, from Vancouver and West Bank, B.C., achieved their first collective agreement as CAW members in 1997, and they were back at the bargaining table. They wanted fair wages, earned sick leave, and scheduling of work and training procedures. Throughout their "unstrike," they continued to work, get paid, and serve customers, but they refused to adhere to the Starbucks dress code, wearing instead whatever they wanted, including their campaign buttons and T-shirts. In November 1999, the CAW members and Starbucks reached a fair resolution and a new two-year agreement.

Workers at six KFC outlets organized their workplaces in Regina last year. The workers—90% of whom are between 17 and 24 years of age—negotiated on the main issues of job security and occupational health and safety. Members of the Hotel and Restaurant Employees Union (HREU) local leafletted every fast food outlet in Regina and also applied for certification at a 7-11 store—a first in Canada.

Discussion Starters:

1. What are the major fast food employers in your community or region? How many jobs do they create? What are the starting wages? What are the working conditions like? Are the jobs temporary, part-time, or full-time?

2. What role do unions play for workers? Why would being members of a union be advantageous? If you're working in retail, is your job organized? Have you ever contemplated approaching a union? What issues would arise in the workplace if you did seek out a union?

3. What steps have been taken in your workplace, or community, to raise awareness about working conditions and rights? What is the role of the employer, and the role of the government in enforcing laws and regulations to ensure that workers' rights are honoured? What improvements could lead to better working conditions in the food services sector?

Resource Materials:

Featherstone, Liza. "The Burger International." Available on the Internet at: www.paniz.com/~dhenwood/McDonalds.html

Livesey, Bruce. "McJob Hell: Young Workers contend with low pay, lousy hours and creepy bosses." *Eye Magazine,* Toronto, June 24, 1999.

Milette, Lisa, as told to Deborah DeAngelis: "Just Because We're Young." *Our Times Magazine.* Vol. 20 No. 1. February/March 2001.

4-d. Work Safety

Young workers are among the most vulnerable of all workers. For many, getting their foot in the door is hard enough. And once they get in, they are faced with a host of new challenges, such as developing new skills, and most are happy just to have a job. They should not have to worry, as well, about being injured on the job. But statistics show that the workplace injury rate is disproportionately higher among young people than for any other group of workers. In 1998, 61,620 workers between the ages of 15 and 24 were injured at their workplaces in Canada, and for 57 of them the injuries proved fatal. Most injuries sustained by young workers occur during their first six months on the job.

The rate of injury has dropped since the mid-1990s, but it is still far too high. Workers as young as 14 have reported injuries on the job. It is essential for young workers to work safely, but the responsibility for a safe workplace does not rest on their shoulders. A survey conducted by the International Accident and Prevention Association (IAPA) found that 56% of young workers reported receiving no safety training before starting new jobs. Nearly one in four (24%) of young workers reported 'near misses' at work, narrowly avoiding injury. Another 19% said they were ex-posed to hazardous materials, and 10% said they had been asked to perform a task they felt was dangerous.

Employers have a responsibility to provide orientation and training to workers, to ensure they are well prepared for their jobs. Young workers need additional support in making safe and healthy choices and avoiding injury while at work. Government legislation exists right across the country to promote workplace health and safety, but, as governments weaken or fail to enforce these protective measures, workers' lives are put at risk. A regular and thorough monitoring of health and safety standards occurs in less than 1% of Canadian workplaces.

In 1999, following the death of David Ellis, an Ontario high school student killed at work on the second day of his job, the bakery for which he worked was fined $75,000. One of the co-owners was sentenced to 20 days in jail, the other fined $7,500. Throughout Ontario history, there have only been three cases in which employers have been sentenced to jail terms for violations of the province's Occupational Health and Safety Act.

Violations of health and safety standards are occurring right now, as you read this page, but the penalties imposed on companies and employers—on those rare occasions when they are charged and found guilty—are not nearly as stringent as they would have to be to compel employers to improve the safety standards and practices in their workplaces. So the lives and physical well-being of workers—especially young workers—continue to be at risk. And the toll of workplace deaths and injuries will not be reduced unless occupational health and safety laws and rules are toughened and strictly enforced—and the penalties for violating them made much more severe.

Quick Facts:

▶ More than six young workers are hurt on the job every hour of every day. Across Canada, given the number of young people employed, that's 60,8000 young workers injured in one year.

▶ Every 15 minutes, each working day, a young worker in British Columbia is injured.

▶ Every day, 50 young workers are injured on the job in Ontario—over 18,000 injuries a year.

▶ In 1998, more than 9,000 workers in Alberta were injured in their first six months on the job. One-third of them were under 25 years old.

▶ Most workplace injuries among young workers occur in food services. Retail stores also have a high injury rate.

▶ The top five causes of injuries include: slips and falls; overexertion; being struck by or against an object; bodily reaction from toxic effects from chemicals; and burns.

▶ Common injuries include: sprains and strains, back injuries; soft tissue injuries such as cuts, punctures and bruises; bone fractures; inflammation of joints; burns or scalds.

Discussion Starters:

1. What are the rights and responsibilities of young workers with respect to health and safety and protection on the job? What are the rights and responsibilities of employers?

2. What action should be taken to make workplaces safer for young workers? What tools, resources and services exist to provide young workers with information and the means for protecting themselves?

3. What is the role of unions, governments, employers, and the community in ensuring that workplaces are safe for young workers?

4. How has government legislation governing workplace health and safety for young workers been weakened or reinforced?

Resource Materials:

Know Your Rights. A Guide to Ontario's Workplace. Centre for Research on Work and Society. York University, November 1998.

Hargrove, Buzz. "Dying to Work." *Globe and Mail* Commentary, July 18, 2000.

Health and Safety on the Job: A Guide for Young Workers. United Steelworkers of America - Ontario and the Workers' Health and Safety Centre. 2000.

Young Workers and Workplace Injuries. Workers' Compensation Board of British Colombia. May 2000.

Young Worker Awareness Program. Workplace Safety and Insurance Board. 1999.

PART III

EXPOSING
CORPORATE
RULE

CANADA
&
WORLD

5. IN CANADA

Through our work in Operation 2000, we have found that youth activists today are deeply concerned about the future of Canada in an age of economic globalization. They understand that there are connections between the forces that are shaping their lives and those that are determining the direction of the country. Often the question is asked: "Who's really in charge? The politicians we elect to represent us? Or the CEOs of the transnational corporations?"

Over the past quarter century, there has been a quiet but determined move on the part of Big Business to gain control over the policy-making machinery of this country, both in Ottawa and in the provincial capitals. Throughout Canada's history, Big Business has always exerted a considerable amount of power over policy-making at federal and provincial levels. But in the mid-1970s, when the influence of Big Business began to wane, a concerted campaign was launched to establish a firmer and more systematic control over policy-making. Powerful business organizations, like the Business Council on National Issues, composed of the CEOs from the 150 largest corporations in the country, were formed for the express purpose of changing the direction of public policy-making and re-inventing the role of government.

During the past 15 years or so, the BCNI and its member corporations have had a profound influence in restructuring Canada's economic and social order. Virtually operating as a shadow cabinet behind the scenes in Ottawa and the provincial capitals, they established a new direction in public policy making—from privatization and deregulation to free trade, the deficit, and tax reform. In doing so, they were successful in re-inventing the role of government in this country, particularly in relation to the policy issues that most directly affect people's daily lives: job creation, health care, social programs, and the environment. In effect, the role of government has been remade in the image of the corporation. So, too, has Canada itself.

The signs of these trends are now woven into the fabric of our culture as a people and a nation—from the predominance of corporate logos and branding to the heavy emphasis of market-oriented values and principles in our common language. Throughout our politics, the private sector has been designated as the prime engine of social as well as economic development and well-being. Increasingly, we find ourselves living in a society where virtually everything is up for sale, including those areas of life once deemed to be a sacred trust—like air and water, seeds and genes, health and education, heritage and culture. The very idea of preserving these and other vital areas of our common life through the public sector is rapidly becoming passé in the politics that governs this country.

For today's youth, there are burning questions about what it means to participate in Canadian society at a time when people are losing their basic democratic rights and freedoms as citizens. How can young people gain control over their economic, social and ecological future in the Canada of McWorld? What does it mean to fight for our democratic rights and freedoms in this age of corporate globalization? The following are just a few of the 'hot button' issues in Canada which pose both a challenge and an opportunity for concerned youth.

5-a. Tax cuts/Role of Government

One of the major issues on the public agenda today is "tax cuts." In the 1990s, Canadians were told that they had to drastically cut back on public services, like education, in order to tackle the problem of Canada's debt and deficit. Now that government deficits have been licked, however, Big Business and its political allies are campaigning for massive tax cuts.

The tax cut campaign is based on the highly charged assumption that "everybody hates paying taxes." But paying taxes, whether we like it or not, is a real and inescapable 'fact of life.' If we want and expect essential public services, then we must pay for them. The only way that governments can provide the basic services that all people need in our society is through revenues collected by taxes.

So, as the 'great tax debate' unfolds, it is important for concerned youth to determine what we get for those taxes, compared with other countries. It is true, for example, that Canadian governments collect taxes that amount to a higher portion of GDP than do U.S. governments. But we also get a great deal more in public services, especially in terms of universal health care and, to a large extent, education, particularly post-secondary education. Indeed, the differences in taxes paid as a percentage of GDP between Canada and the U.S. disappears, says a Standard & Poors DRI study, once expenditures for Medicare and education are added to total government receipts.

What's more, Canadians pay less in taxes as a percentage of GDP than do citizens in most European countries. But Europeans also get more public services and social programs in return. In many European countries, there are publicly-funded programs that provide universal child care services, university education (with low or no tuition fees), maternity leave with adequate pay for all working mothers, and a much more comprehensive insurance program for unemployed workers.

As one of Canada's best known tax policy experts, Neil Brooks, puts it: "Taxes are the price we pay for a more civilized society." What those who campaign for tax cuts want

Quick Facts:

▶ In their sales pitch, business campaigners argue that tax cuts will provide "relief" for ordinary citizens. But, according to a *Statistics Canada* study measuring the percentage of Canadian household budgets spent on four basic items (food, shelter, transportation, and personal income taxes), it is only for the top two-fifths of income earners that taxes are the major household expenditure.

▶ Among the 29 industrialized countries in the OECD, Canada is ranked in the middle of the pack, with total tax revenue amounting to 36.8% of our GDP. Fourteen countries collect more and 14 countries less as a percentage of their GDP than does Canada.

▶ A key benchmark for assessing the tax burden is 'disposable income' or income after taxes. For a family with two children, Canada's average disposable income is 81.8%, 3.3% below the OECD average in 1996. Canada's disposable income rate was even slightly higher than the U.S. rate that year.

▶ According to a study, Canada has the lowest effective corporate income tax rate among major industrialized countries. Conducted in 1997 by KPMG, a leading international accounting and management consulting firm, the study compared the costs of doing business in seven countries (i.e., the U.S., U.K., France, Germany, Italy, Sweden, and Canada). Canada's rate was 27.4% compared with the U.S. at 40%.

▶ Canada's payroll taxes, which are often portrayed as 'job killers' because they are paid by all companies with employees, are actually 25% less than the OECD average. In comparison with the U.S., Canada's payroll taxes are 30% lower.

▶ In these times of government surpluses, polls reveal that most Canadians, when given the choice, prefer that additional revenues go towards needs like health care, education, child poverty, job creation, child care and debt reduction, rather than tax cuts. In late 1996, a *Globe and Mail*/Environics poll showed that only 9% of Canadians wanted tax cuts, while 31% wanted surpluses to go towards job creation, 25% to health care, and 13% to addressing child poverty.

is to permanently downsize government and drastically reduce public services. This is what the tax cut debate is really all about. Do we want a civilized society where basic services that are needed by all people are provided on a universal basis by our governments through publicly-funded and administered programs? That's the key question.

To challenge the campaigners for tax cuts, however, does not imply that the current tax system is fair. There are plenty of grounds to argue otherwise. As long as wealthy Canadians and profitable corporations continue to get away with not paying their fair share of taxes in this country, the tax system itself will be unfair and in need of change. But this calls for a different kind of public debate than one simply based on whether there should be major tax cuts.

Resource Materials:

Brooks, Neil. *Paying for a Civilized Society,* Canadian Centre for Policy Alternatives. Ottawa, 1995/96

Canadian Centre for Policy Alternatives and CHOICES: A Coalition for Social Justice, *Healthy Families: First Things First. Alternative Federal Budget 2000.* Canadian Centre for Policy Alternatives, Ottawa, 2000.

Dobbin, Murray. *Ten Tax Myths*, Canadian Centre for Policy Alternatives, Ottawa, October, 1999.

KPMG, *The Comparative Alternative: A comparison of business costs in Canada, Europe and the United States.* Prospectus Inc., October, 1997.

Ontario Coalition for Social Justice et. al., *Unfair Shares: Corporations and Taxation in Canada.* An annual report published in collaboration with the Ontario Federation of Labour based on data provided by the InfoGlobe's Report on Business Corporate Database.

Discussion Starters:

1. How important is the issue of 'tax cuts' for youth today? Is it a real concern? How often does the issue arise in conversations among young people? To what extent do they see that taxes are the price that people must pay for a more civilized society?

2. What kinds of public services do governments (federal, provincial, municipal) provide which are of key importance to young people now? Public education? Post-secondary education? Job creation? Health care? What impacts could tax cuts have on the ability of governments to provide these public services? What about other kinds of public services that may be needed in the future?

3. What actions have been taken to address these issues in your university or college? your workplace? or your high school? What further initiatives could be taken to build greater public awareness and action on these issues?

5-b. Food Safety - Frankenfoods

Critics call them "frankenfoods." They come from crops and animals that have been genetically modified (GM) or engineered. Unbeknownst to most Canadians, GM food products have been quietly and quickly making their way onto the dinner tables in our homes and restaurants, radically changing the quality of what we eat.

Close to 75% of all prepackaged food is now estimated to contain genetically modified substances. Most of the main staples in our food chain—corn, soya, potatoes, canola—are now grown with GM substances, mixed with regularly grown crops and then processed into food products that appear at our supermarkets. Aided by scorpion genes, for example, corn can be grown with a built-in pesticide. Today, the products of GM-grown crops include virtually everything from breakfast cereals to salad dressing to french fries and infant formula.

The manufacturers of GM food products claim that they are perfectly safe for human consumption and friendly to the environment. But some scientists at Health Canada have expressed serious concerns about food safety and the lack of long-term testing to determine the impacts of GM food products on human health. Without long-term testing, people with food allergies are particularly in danger of being put in harm's way. At the same time, environmentalists have shown that GM crops in farmers' fields do run the risk of increasing rather than decreasing pesticide use, while others have warned about the prospects of generating super-weeds and super-pests as byproducts. Nor is it clear what will happen when GM crops cross-pollinate with other plants.

In Europe, widespread public uncertainty and resistance to GM foods has compelled governments to place bans on some genetically modified crops and foods, while some grocery store chains, restaurants and fast food retailers have refused to sell these products. Here in Canada, public opinion polls consistently show that 75% of Canadians who are familiar with GM foods are worried about their safety. The same polls conclude that 95% want all GM foods on the market to be labelled.

So far, however, Ottawa has refused to take any action in response to this growing public demand for mandatory labelling, let alone placing a moratorium or a ban on certain GM food products. After all, Canada is one of the leading promoters of biotechnology and exporters of GM products. In its push to open up new markets for GM crops and food products in Europe, the Canadian government joined the U.S. and the major biotech corporations in getting the World Trade Organization to declare Europe's safety ban on hormone-treated beef from North America to be illegal under the WTO trade rules.

Quick Facts:

▶ *Canada is among the world's leading growers and producers of GM crops. In terms of staple crops alone, 57% of all the canola, 45% of the corn, and 25% of the soya grown in this country is genetically modified.*

▶ *Many of the major biotech corporations on the cutting edge of GM food products—Monsanto (now the Pharmacia Corporation), DuPont, Dow—have highly questionable track records in the chemical and pharmaceutical industry. Monsanto has been the producer of toxic PCBs, as well as Agent Orange used for bio-warfare purposes in the Vietnam war. DuPont has produced weapons-grade plutonium and leaded gas, while Dow is known for its manufacturing of Napalm and silicon breast implants.*

▶ *When Canadian farmers plant Monsanto's GM crops, they are required to sign a "technology use agreement" which makes it legally binding for them to continue purchasing Monsanto Round-Up Ready products. Farmers who fail to abide by these rules can expect to be sued by Monsanto.*

▶ *In addition to showing that 95% of Canadians familiar with GM food products want them to be labelled as such, the same poll conducted by the Environics Research Group on behalf of the Council of Canadians showed that 95% also want consumers to be able to have the choice to buy non-GM foods in their grocery stores. What's more, 71% say they would be prepared to pay higher prices for non-GM food products, if necessary.*

▶ *While grocery retailers say they depend on the Canadian government's testing and approval procedures for GM products on the market, the same Environics poll showed that 56% of Canadians familiar with GM foods had little or no confidence in Ottawa's ability to adequately protect them when it comes to insuring the health and safety of GM food products. Furthermore, an Angus Reid poll found that two-thirds of Canadians would be less likely to buy food labelled as genetically modified.*

Resistance/Activities:

In January 2000, the Biosafety Protocol Conference was held in Montreal, where delegates demonstrated in the streets against the global trade of genetically modified living organisms. As a result, the Biosafety Protocol adopted at this conference recognized the right and responsibility of governments to regulate the imports of GMOs, including genetically modified foods. Since then, the Council of Canadians and Greenpeace have mounted campaigns demanding that grocery store chains like Loblaws become GM-free in terms of the food products they sell.

At the same time, bio-justice activists have been gathering in various cities around the world to protest against the biotechnology companies at their conventions. In June 2001, for example, bio-justice activists organized a counter-conference at a major biotech industry conference in San Diego, California. Direct action protests were staged in the city's streets, along with solidarity action in communities across the U.S. and Canada.

Meanwhile, youth activists in the bio-justice movement have led the way in organizing direct action resistance at field-test sites for GM food crops. From the UK and France to India and Brazil, young bio-justice activists have risked being arrested and jailed by organizing campaigns to destroy GM crops at test sites.

Discussion Starters:

1. What concerns do youth have about the safety and quality of genetically modified foods? To what extent are GM foods an issue in schools, on campus, in the workplace, or the community? What does it mean for the youth of today to be the first generation of a biotech age?

2. What policies and laws should be adopted by the federal government on GM foods? Should all manufacturers of GM food products be required to label and identify their ingredients? Should a moratorium be called on the sale of some GM food products until long-term testing has been done? Are there some biotech and genetically modified products that should be banned altogether?

3. What needs to be done to get our politicians to take action on these fronts? What measures should be taken to regulate or control the operations of the biotech industry? What role can be played by youth?

Resource Materials:

Boyens, Ingeborg. *Unnatural Harvest: How Corporate Science is Secretly Altering Our Food.* Doubleday Canada, Toronto, 1999.

The Council of Canadians, *The Facts on GM Foods*. A set of fact-sheets on: "What are genetically modified foods?" "Should genetically modified foods be labelled?" and "Who's behind genetically modified foods?"

The Council of Canadians, *Get It Off The Shelf!* A handbook for organizing a campaign to get Loblaws to go GM-free.

Kneen, Brewster. *Farmageddon: Food and the Culture of Biotechnology.* New Society Publishers, Gabriola Island, 1999.

Rifkin, Jeremy. *The Biotech Century: Harnessing the Gene and Remaking the World.* Tarcher/Putnam Books, New York, 1998.

5-c. Health Care

Our universally accessible, publicly-funded and administered health care—enshrined in the Canada Health Act—is often referred to as the crown jewel of social programs that distinguishes who we are as a nation. But whether this crown jewel will be passed on intact to present and future generations of youth is at least an open question. For not only has health care become cash-strapped due to massive cuts in federal transfer payments to the provinces through the 1995 Canada Health and Social Transfer Act, but key parts of the system are now in danger of being privatized and taken over by for-profit corporations.

Over the past decade or so, a powerful for-profit health care industry has been built up in the U.S. When President Clinton tried to bring in a modified form of public health care during his first term in office, he was effectively blocked by this industry. From the perspective of the U.S. corporations, Canada's health care system represents a $76-billion-a-year market. The more that cash-starved provincial health care plans delist medical services and allow for the privatization of health care, the more the doors are opened to foreign-based, for-profit corporations.

The alarm bells sounded in late 1999 when Alberta introduced legislation permitting hospital services, including services now publicly insured, to be contracted out to private for-profit companies. The Alberta plan was viewed by critics as not only violating the governing principles of the Canada Health Act, but also paving the way for a two-tiered health care system. According to legal experts, the Alberta legislation would allow U.S.-based health care corporations to use the North American Free Trade Agreement (NAFTA) to gain access to public funds for their operations in the province (despite the fact that health care is exempted as a public service from the NAFTA rules). The Alberta law would also make it difficult for other provinces to protect their public health insurance plans.

Indeed, the Ontario government had already begun to open the doors of its public health care system by allowing American for-profit corporations to establish facilities for a wide range of services, from cataract surgery to abortions and kidney dialysis. While the takeover of Ontario's non-profit Blue Cross by Liberty Mutual, a U.S.-based for-profit company, signalled this trend, corporations like

Kaiser (the second largest health insurance company in the U.S.) have specifically targeted Canada as a major growth market. Moreover, Canada's private insurance companies (e.g., London Life, Manulife, Great West Life) were bound to benefit from the delisting of medically insured services from the Ontario Health Insurance Plan and the introduction of user fees.

Quick Facts:

▶ Following a strong lobbying campaign in 1993, the giants of the transnational pharmaceutical industry succeeded in gaining monopoly protection over their drug patents in this country—a monopoly that was later cemented in the intellectual property rights sections of NAFTA.

▶ As a result, drug prices have skyrocketed, reaping profits for the major pharmaceutical transnationals (e.g., Eli Lilly, Merck, Pfizer, and Bristol-Myers), while Canada's own generic drug industry (which used to reproduce patented pharmaceutical products at reasonable prices) has been damaged.

▶ In May 2000, the World Trade Organization (WTO) further ruled that Canada's patent protection period for different drugs is insufficient and must be extended, thereby adding another $200 million in costs to consumers and provincial health care plans over the next few years.

▶ Among the major privateers of health care in Canada are the world's largest management consultant firm, KPMG (whose Toronto office is headed by the same people who masterminded the drive to privatize hospitals in London, England) and a Canadian-owned corporation, MDS, which has been a major player in private health care, providing services to over 17,000 physicians and institutions in seven provinces.

▶ MDS is also poised to act as a midwife for foreign-based corporations in the health care field seeking markets in Canada by forming joint ventures with the world's largest hospital chain, Columbia/HCA, and with Bristol Myers Squibb, the pharmaceutical giant.

▶ U.S.-based companies like Kaiser Permenante and Aetna Health Care Inc. may also lead the way in promoting the introduction of Home Maintenance Organizations (HMOs) which have mushroomed as a key component of the for-profit American health care industry over the past decade.

▶ The inclusion of health care in the current WTO negotiations on trade in cross-border services means that Canada will likely be facing a new set of global trade rules designed to reinforce the rights of for-profit health care corporations and their operations in this country.

Discussion Starters:

1. What kind of health care system do young people want to see in Canada? Should we allow health care to become a profit-making industry based on the ability to pay? Or should we fight to preserve and enhance a universally accessible, publicly-funded and administered health care system based on people's needs?

2. Who are some of the key corporate players promoting the privatization and commercialization of health care in your province? What parts of Medicare appear to be most vulnerable? What groups are researching and tracking these trends, and how do we connect with them?

3. What are some of the potential concerns and issues regarding the corporate takeover of health care services in your community? What can be done to build local resistance around these issues? How can concerned youth become more actively involved?

Resistance/Activities:

The fight for the preservation of universal health care in Canada is about to shift into fast gear. When Alberta introduced legislation (Bill 11) allowing publicly-insured hospital services to be contracted out to private, for-profit companies, a group called Friends of Medicare began holding vigils in 2000 outside the provincial legislature. Soon the vigils mushroomed into a province-wide protest against the Klein government's measures to privatize health care. While they were unable to stop the bill from being enacted, Friends of Medicare succeeded in establishing a solid base of public resistance against the move towards a two-tiered health care system—one for the rich and one for the poor—in this country.

By mid-2001, the resistance escalated as overworked and underpaid nurses walked off the job in two other provinces, British Columbia and Nova Scotia, because of the failure of these governments to provide adequate support for both patients and care-givers. This kind of resistance is bound to continue, not only because of inadequate government funding, but also because of the new threats to Medicare posed by NAFTA, the GATS, and other WTO trade agreements that would open the door to more corporate takeovers of health care services.

Resource Materials:

Armstrong, Hugh, Pat Armstrong and David Coburn. *The Political Economy of Health and Health Care in Canada.* Oxford University Press, Toronto 2000.

Fuller, Colleen. "Caring for profit." *Canadian Forum,* June, 1998.

Fuller, Colleen. *Caring for Profit: How Multinationals Are Taking Over Canada's Health Care Sector.* CCPA/New Star publication, Ottawa, 1998.

Lexchin, Dr. Noel. *A National Pharmacare Plan: Combining Efficiency and Equity.* CCPA, Ottawa, March 2001.

Sanger, Matthew. *Reckless Abandon: Canada, the GATS, and the Future of Health Care.* CCPA, Ottawa, February 2001.

5-d. Green Machine

More than any other generation before, today's youth are both deeply conscious of and concerned about the future of the environment. At the dawn of the 21ˢᵗ century, the signs of an ecological holocaust are looming on the horizon—from global warming, climate change, and the destruction of bio-diversity, to the depletion of our forests, rivers, streams and fish stocks.

According to the Intergovernmental Panel on Climate Change, composed of 2,500 scientists from around the world, the Earth is on the verge of massive climate changes due to greenhouse gas emissions that are more than likely to result in "significant loss of life." The main cause, they say, is the burning of fossil fuels (oil, coal, gas, etc.) which, in turn, generate and emit greenhouse gases into the lower atmosphere, thereby trapping heat near the Earth's surface. With this trapped heat comes higher temperatures and rising sea levels, leading to more droughts, floods, and the spread of infectious diseases.

The looming problem of global warming is exacerbated by the potential collapse of the Earth's lungs through the rapid depletion of the planet's major forests. Canada's boreal forests constitute over one-third of the planet's northern lung. According to a report of the World Resources Institute and Global Forest Watch, Canada is setting the stage for a major ecological setback by allowing logging companies to clear-cut old growth and other prime trees in the northern boreal forests.

The world is also facing a massive crisis in fresh water. Worldwide, the consumption of water is doubling every 20 years. By the year 2025, two-thirds of the world's population will be living in conditions of serious water shortage, half of them in conditions of absolute water scarcity. Since Canada's lakes and rivers contain the world's largest supply of fresh water, there are mounting demands to harness this resource for bulk exports and sale, despite the ecological havoc that this would cause.

Instead of providing the strong environmental leadership that is desperately needed, Ottawa and the provinces have largely danced to the tune of the major resource industries. Government environmental policy task forces are dominated by industry representatives. Take, for example, the federal task force on greenhouse gas emissions, which was to come up with a plan for Canada to meet the Kyoto reduction targets. Due mainly to resistance by representatives of the petroleum industry, the task force has failed to agree on a plan four years after the Kyoto summit. Or take Ottawa's recently passed Environment Protection Act, which was weakened and declawed as brand name corporations like Alcan, Noranda, Dow Chemical, Stelco, and Procter & Gamble, along with their industry associations, lined up their fire power to drastically dilute what was already a weak environmental bill.

Reports show that government capacity for environmental protection has also been seriously damaged by the deregulation and downsizing that has taken place in recent years. In Ontario, for example, the Ontario Institute for Environmental Law has documented how much of the provincial machinery for environmental regulation has been dismantled by downsizing. A classic case is the failure of the Ontario Ministry of the Environment to deal with the E.coli contamination of the water supply in Walkerton, despite early warnings before the outbreak in the spring of 2000. Nor is this the only case. When a toxic fire broke out in Hamilton, the Ontario Ministry of the Environment had to rely on essential information from Greenpeace because it lacked the resources required to analyze and respond to such an serious pollution crisis.

Quick Facts:

▶ The world's leading scientists on the Intergovernmental Panel on Climate Change predict that the rate of global warming will be "greater than any seen in the last 10,000 years." To stabilize the Earth's climate, the Panel maintains that cuts in greenhouse gas emissions of 50-to-70% below 1990 levels will be required. This is a far cry from the Kyoto Agreement, which calls for an average reduction level of 5.2% below 1990 emission levels by 2008-2012.

▶ According to the report of the World Resources Institute and Global Forest Watch, the logging tenures granted by federal and provincial governments to timber corporations harvesting on Crown land now cover half of Canada's boreal forests, for a total land mass of 529 million hectares. The report says that 90% of logging in Canada is now focused on old growth and primary forests, primarily in the form of clear-cutting.

▶ More than half of all cancers are caused by exposure to carcinogenic substances in the environment. While the most obvious of these substances is tobacco smoke, many chemicals found in the workplace, such as benzene, asbestos, chromium, coal tars and PCBs (to name a few) can be environmentally hazardous to peoples' health. It has been estimated that the annual production of chemicals, many of which are carcinogenic, increased from one billion pounds in 1940 to over 500 billion pounds a year by the 1990s.

▶ According to the United Nations Food and Agriculture Organization (FAO), close to 70% of the world's fisheries have been over-fished. In the last 30 years, the number of fishing vessels has nearly doubled. So, too, has the registered tonnage of fish caught, from 13 million tonnes in 1970 to over 26 million in the 1990s. The big trawlers are largely responsible for the huge increase. The 40,000 largest ocean-bound fishing ships catch as much as 3.4 million smaller boats in the coastal waters.

Discussion Starters:

1. What are some of the burning environmental issues for concerned youth today? In your community, your school, your campus, or your workplace? What concerns do young people have about major environmental threats like global warming, forestry depletion, and water scarcity? What about air pollution and toxic wastes?

2. Name some of the key corporations in each sector or industry? What role did they play in promoting environmental deregulations? What kinds of profit margins do these corporations have? What has been their record in paying corporate taxes? What cash contributions have they made to the governing party?

3. What are the dangers of lowering environmental standards and allowing the corporations in each industry to self-regulate themselves, rather than be regulated by government? What has been done in your community to build public awareness and actions around these issues? What more could be done?

Resistance/Activities:

Around the world, environmental activists have been taking to the streets in protest against global warming and climate change. When U.S. President George W. Bush met with European leaders in Stockholm in June 2001, mass demonstrations were organized to protest the U.S. rejection of the Kyoto Accord.

Elsewhere, groups like Friends of the Earth and Greenpeace International have mounted campaigns against oil giants like Exxon, Mobil, and British Petroleum for the role they play in the fossil fuel industry as prime agents of global warming.

In Canada, the David Suzuki Foundation and the Sierra Club have also organized protests against the Canadian government for failing to take effective action on global warming.

In the 1990s, youth activists played a major role in campaigns to block the clearcut logging of old-growth forests near Clayquot Sound in British Columbia. Today, environmental activists, including many young people, are engaged in struggles to maintain community control over the depletion of scarce water supplies. In Bolivia, for example, hundreds of thousands participated in mass protests against the corporate takeover of local water services in the spring of 2000, while in Canada the Council of Canadians has led the way in organizing resistance against bulk exports of water.

Resource Materials:

Barlow, Maude. *Blue Gold.* The International Forum on Globalization, 2000.

Ontario Institute for Environmental Law. *Ontario's Law and the Common Sense Revolution.* Ontario Institute for Environmental Law, Toronto, 1998.

Sierra Club of Canada. *Rio + 9: The Ninth Annual Rio Report Card.* Sierra Club of Canada, Ottawa, 2001.

Sierra Club of Canada. "Global Warming and the Circumpolar Region." Sierra Club of Canada, Ottawa, 2000.

Sierra Youth Coalition. "Doing Your Bit." Sierra Youth Coalition, Ottawa, 2001. (See also www.thebit.ca)

5-e. Mediasaurus

In any democratic society, the media plays a pivotal role in determining the quality of public discussion and debate. As Noam Chomsky has repeatedly demonstrated, public consent around major policy issues is something which is often "manufactured" by the media for those who govern and rule. A key factor in "manufacturing consent" is who owns and controls the major newspapers, television, and radio organizations.

In recent years, Canada's media have become increasingly dominated by a handful of corporate moguls like Conrad Black, Ken Thomson, Paul Desmarais, Ted Rogers, and Izzy Asper. Instead of keeping Canadians well informed about public issues and stimulating debate from diverse political perspectives, there has been a growing tendency for the mainstream media to act as a mouthpiece for the corporate agenda in this country.

Media analyst James Winter of Windsor University has shown through case studies that those who own and control the media today exercise a great deal of influence over news content. This influence is exerted, says Winter, not only through hiring and firing practices with regards to reporters, but also by decisions affecting the placement and editing of news stories.

As Conrad Black's own right-hand man at Hollinger Inc., David Radler, once put it: "The buck stops with the ownership. I am responsible for meeting the payroll, therefore I will ultimately determine what the newspapers say and how they're going to be run." It is not surprising, therefore, that many open-minded journalists (who, after all, are workers themselves with individual and family responsibilities) often feel they have to fall in line or join the ranks of the unemployed. The prolonged strike in 1999 by workers at the *Calgary Herald* served to bring these issues to public attention across the country.

During the mid-1990s, the wave of consolidations and merger mania that swept through the U.S. media industry raised major alarm bells. Each of the big U.S. broadcasting networks was taken over by a corporate giant from another industry. CNN was bought out by Time-Warner, NBC by General Electric, CBS by Westinghouse, and ABC by the Disney Corporation. Then the AOL and Time-Warner merger in 2000 set the stage for creating the largest media communications empire, linking film, broadcasting and the emerging Internet industries into one huge conglomerate.

Here in Canada, there has been a similar wave of consolidations in the media industry during the same period. In 1996, Conrad Black's Hollinger Corporation seized control of the Southam chain of newspapers, thereby becoming majority owner of nearly 60% of all the daily circulation in Canada. Then, in a move reminiscent of the AOL/Time-Warner merger, Canada's telecommunication giant, BCE, bought CTV, Canada's main private television company, thereby establishing a new media conglomerate linking broadcasting and the Internet. And, more recently, Izzy Asper's CanWest Global Communications made a successful bid to purchase the lion's share of Hollinger's major metropolitan newspapers, thus potentially taking over the lead in the race to become Canada's dominant provider of Internet information.

These consolidations are bound to intensify pressures for the privatization of Canada's public broadcasting system. With all the hype about how "costly, inefficient and wasteful" the CBC is, the stage is being set for the corporate takeover of public broadcasting. Despite the fact that the CBC itself sometimes acts as a mouthpiece for the corporate agenda, it has traditionally served as a vehicle for the expression of public dissent and democratic debate.

Quick Facts:

▶ In the late 1950s, the Southam and Thomson newspaper chains owned 25% of all daily circulation in the country. By 1970, their control had risen to 45%, and a Special Senate Committee on Media Concentration began to ring alarm bells.

▶ In 1980, the Kent Royal Commission on Newspapers reported that three major chains (Southam, Thomson, *Toronto Star*) controlled 57% of daily circulation. By 1995, these three chains controlled 77% of the dailies (67% by Southam and Thomson, and 10% by the *Toronto Star*). At the same time, Paul Desmarais owned four major newspapers in Quebec, while the Irvings controlled all the newspapers in New Brunswick.

▶ In 1996, Conrad Black's Hollinger corporation seized control of Southam and suddenly became the single largest owner of Canada's newspapers. With the Southam takeover, Black owned and controlled 64 out of 104 daily newspapers, reaching more than 2.3 million households every day across the country. His media empire encompassed all the dailies in Saskatchewan, Newfoundland and P.E.I., along with two-thirds of all the daily newspapers in Ontario.

▶ By becoming the majority owner of Southam, Black also gained effective control over Canadian Press, which provides news services to small-town newspapers and radio stations across Canada in both official languages. It also appeared that Black's move to launch the *National Post* in 1998 was not only designed to rival but potentially to replace the *Globe and Mail* as Canada's national newspaper.

▶ In 2000 came the $3.5 billion takeover by Izzy Asper's CanWest Global Communications of Hollinger's stable of major metropolitan newspapers, including the *Calgary Herald, Edmonton Journal, Montreal Gazette, Ottawa Citizen* and the *Vancouver Sun*, plus a 50% stake in the *National Post*. As a major Canadian broadcaster in its own right, CanWest is now in a position—as one business commentator described it—"to put a stranglehold on Canadian content that can then be used on the Internet". After all, CanWest's string of new acquisitions provides the capacity for local news and information gathering needed for effective use of the Internet.

Discussion Starters:

1. What are some of the concerns you have about increasing corporate ownership and control of the media in this country? Can you identify specific examples where news coverage has been biased or ignored because of influence exerted by big corporate owners?

2. To what extent are youth concerned about the concentration of corporate ownership and control over vital media sectors such as newspapers, broadcasting, and the Internet? Should one or two big corporations be allowed to dominate these sectors of Canada's media? What negative impacts could this have on the quality of democracy in this country? What measures should be taken by Ottawa to regulate corporate mergers and takeovers in Canada's media industry?

3. Are there any concrete examples of corporate control of the media in your community or region? If so, what has been or is being done to raise public awareness and actions around this issue? What kinds of alternative forms of media are available in your region? What steps, if any, are being taken to support and strengthen these alternatives?

Resistance/Activities:

In Canada and elsewhere, resistance against the corporate-dominated media has taken many different forms. The strike by the Calgary Herald *workers in 1999-2000 served to highlight some of the harsh employment practices of media moguls like Conrad Black. But young people today often find themselves "tuning-out" the established media as a form of resistance.*

Increasingly, young people are turning to independent and alternative media centres that have been created all over the world, from Canada to countries like Mexico and Colombia in Latin America, as well as in countries throughout Europe. Here in Canada, for example, the Canadian Centre for Policy Alternatives publishes a monthly newsletter, The CCPA Monitor, *that appeals to many young people, as well as numerous books and studies that provide progressive news and views not usually found in the commercial media. As well, independent on-line web-sites, like the CCPA's (*www.policyalternatives.ca*),* rabble.ca, straightgoods, *and* flipside, *are more and more being used as alternative and progressive sources.*

Resource Materials:

Barlow, Maude, and James Winter. *The Big Black Book: The Essential Views of Conrad and Barbara Amiel Black,* Stoddart Books, Toronto, 1997.

Hackett, Robert, and Richard Gruneau. *The Missing News: Filters and Blind Spots in Canada's Press.* Canadian Centre for Policy Alternatives and Garamond Press, Ottawa, 2000.

Herman, Edward, and Robert McChesney. *The Global Media: The New Missionaries of Global Capitalism.* Cassell, London, 1997.

Winter, James. *Democracy's Oxygen: How Corporations Control the News.* Black Rose Books, Montreal, 1997.

Wolf, Michael J. *The Entertainment Economy: How Mega Media Forces Are Transforming Our Lives.* Random House, New York, 1999.

6. AROUND THE WORLD

As the battles of Seattle, Washington, Prague, Quebec City and Genoa have shown, there is certainly plenty of evidence that increasing numbers of today's youth are becoming deeply concerned about the future of the planet and the driving forces behind corporate-driven globalization.

For better or worse, young people are more and more conscious of the fact that they live in a wired global village where they are instantly bombarded, not only by consumer products and corporate brand names in the marketplace, but by related political issues and events occurring half way around the world. Some have focused their energies on what climate change and global warming are doing to the Earth. Others are joining hands with youth movements in China, Burma, Indonesia and Nigeria to resist ongoing repression of human rights. And still others are trying to spark public awareness of issues ranging from the patenting of human genes to the renewed buildup of the global arms race.

Yet the world that today's youth face in the new millennium changed dramatically during the final quarter of the 20th century. The old world order which emerged from the ashes of the Second World War has been replaced by a new world order. The world that today's parents and grandparents grew up in was char-acterized by a bi-polar global economy, divided between capitalism and communism. For the most part, political decisions about not only economic, but also social, cultural and environmental policy matters, were made in the context of this great ideological divide. However, with the collapse of the Cold War, symbolized by the fall of the Berlin Wall in 1989, capitalism and the market system emerged triumphant.

Today, the market system reigns supreme in the new global economy, with transnational corporations and banks as the dominant institutions. For the most part, global corporations now outstrip most nation states when it comes to wielding economic and political clout. As the political significance of the United Nations has declined, new institutions of economic power like the World Trade Organization have emerged as global governing councils. These new political forces of economic globalization, in turn, are fuelled by a financial casino that transfers trillions of dollars in electronic money around the world every day, aided and abetted by the International Monetary Fund and the World Bank.

Once again, if youth activists are going to take some measure of control over their economic, social and ecological future in the 21st century, it is imperative to come to grips with these new global forces.

6-a. Global Fortune 500

Every year, the world's leading business magazines and newspapers rank the top transnational corporations in terms of their annual revenues, profits, and other indicators of economic power. The best known is the Global Fortune 500 published by *Fortune* magazine in the U.S.

Over the past two decades, the number of transnational corporations has mushroomed. Thirty years ago, the United Nations counted some 7,000. Today, there are over 45,000, with more than 280,000 affiliates around the world. What's more, out of the top 100 economies in the world today, 52 are transnational corporations.

General Motors, currently the largest transnational conglomerate in the world, has more total revenue than all but 23 nation states on this planet. Wal-Mart is larger than the economies of 163 countries. Ford's economy is bigger than either Norway or South Africa. Japan's Mitsui & Co. has annual sales greater than Poland, while Philip Morris's yearly revenues outstrip the Czech Republic and Hungary. Mitsubishi, Shell and Itochu corporations each have annual revenues larger than countries like Saudi Arabia, Finland, or Portugal. And Toyota's annual sales are bigger than countries like Israel, Egypt and Ireland.

The annual sales and profits of the top 200 global corporations have also been outpacing world economic growth. According to the Institute for Policy Studies in Washington, the sales of the top 200 corporations grew 160%, while their profits jumped 224% between 1983 and 1997. During the same period, total world economic growth increased by only 144%. What's more, there has been a tremendous boom in mergers and the concentration of corporate wealth. In 1998, merger deals worth $1.6 trillion were made, a 78% increase over 1997.

At the same time, these transnational corporations can no longer be simply viewed as economic machines alone. They have also become highly sophisticated political machines. In all the major industrialized countries and regions of the world, these corporate giants have organized their own political alliances, such as the Business Round Table in the U.S., the Keidanren in Japan, the Round Table of Industrialists in Europe, and the Business Council on National Issues here in Canada. Their mandate has been not only to institute pro-big-business policies, but also to re-invent government itself. Unelected and unaccountable, these new political machines of transnational corporations have, in effect, mounted an arsenal of powerful weapons (e.g., legal and public relations firms, lobby machinery, political advertising in the media, citizen front groups, plus political party donations) for their campaigns.

Indeed, transnational corporations have emerged as the dominant institutions on this planet. Fortified by telecommunications technology and the global movement of finance capital, transnational corporations are now able to shift production from one country or region to another around the world at a moment's notice, outflanking both nation states and workers' demands.

Discussion Starters:

1. What are some of the dangers of transnational corporations becoming larger and more powerful than nation states? What impacts does this have on peoples' sovereignty?

2. What dangers exist when entire sectors of the global economy are concentrated in the hands of a few TNCs? What happens when TNCs operate as political machines to change public policies and governance structures for their own ends? What does this do to democracy?

3. What has been done to promote public discussion and debate about these issues in your community? What other initiatives could be taken to promote public awareness and action on the growing power of global corporations and the threat to democracy?

Quick Facts:

► The combined sales of the world's top 200 corporations are equal to 26% of the world's Gross National Product, yet these same top 200 conglomerates employ less than three-quarters of one percent of the world's work force.

► Five transnational corporations alone control 50% of the global market in seven industries (i.e., consumer durables, automobiles, airlines, aerospace, electrical components, electrical and electronic, and steel).

► Petroleum production and refining has become largely controlled by 10 majors in the world, five of which are U.S.-based (Exxon, Mobil, Texaco, Chevron, and Amoco), two British (Royal Dutch Shell, British Petroleum), two French (Elf Aquitaine, Total), and one Italian (Eni).

► While many companies worldwide are involved in forest and paper production, the industry is now concentrated in the hands of five majors, four of which are U.S.- based (International Paper, Georgia-Pacific, Kimberly-Clark, and Weyerhaeuser) and one Japanese (Nippon Paper Industries).

► In electronics and electrical equipment, Japanese corporations control seven of the top 10 spots (Hitashi, Matsushita Electric, Toshiba, Sony, NEC, Mitsubishi, Sanyo, and Sharp), followed by two U.S. companies (General Electric, Motorola).

► Wal-Mart has become the world's top retailer with its superstore chains (i.e., selling a wide range of consumer goods like food, clothing, hardware, furniture, pharmaceuticals, etc.), followed by five other U.S. companies, two Japanese firms, one German and one French.

► Other global retailers like Coca Cola, Procter & Gamble, Philip Morris, R.J.R. Nabisco, Kellogg, Unilever, Pepsico, Nestlé, Kentucky Fried Chicken and McDonald's spend billions of dollars on advertising and promotion each year to create a global market based on mass consumption.

Resistance/Activities:

Around the world, there are growing signs that members of the global Fortune 500 are becoming targets of resistance. Corporate research networks, providing on-line information and profiles of major transnational corporations, have sprung up, including Corporate Watch in the U.S., Corporate Watch in the UK, Corporate Europe Observatory in the Netherlands, Transnationale in France, the IBON Institute in the Philippines, and the Polaris Institute in Canada.

In the U.S. and Canada, youth activists have also begun to make effective use of various tools to unmask and expose the operations of major transnational corporations. In anti-sweatshop campaigns, for example, culture-jamming techniques have been used to draw attention to the exploitation of workers by corporations such as Nike and Disney. Corporate bus tours have been organized in Toronto and other urban centres to expose young people to the headquarters of major corporations and the homes of their CEOs, along with running commentaries and information handouts.

In India and elsewhere, local communities have organized to get rid of corporate giants like DuPont, Monsanto, and Coca-Cola. And, in a growing number of U.S. towns, citizens are pressuring their municipal governments to take legislative action on a variety of fronts, such as refusing to recognize corporations as "persons" with rights in their community, setting a limit on the number of chain-stores allowed to operate in the community, and applying the "three-strikes-and-you're-out" approach to prevent any corporation with a criminal record from setting up shop in the community.

Resource Materials:

Anderson, Sarah, and John Cavanagh, with Thea Lee. *Field Guide to the Global Economy.* Institute for Policy Studies, Washington DC, 2000.

Barnet, R., and J. Cavanagh. *Global Dreams: Imperial Corporations and the New World Order.* Simon and Schuster, New York, 1994.

Clarke, Tony. *Silent Coup: Confronting the Big Business Takeover of Canada.* Canadian Centre for Policy Alternatives and James Lorimer & Co., Ottawa, 1997.

Derber, Charles. *Corporation Nation: How Corporations Are Taking Over Our Lives and What Can be Done About It.* St. Martin's/Griffen, New York, 1998.

Dobbin, Murray. *The Myth of the Good Corporate Citizen: Democracy Under the Rule of Big Business.* Stoddart Books, Toronto, 1999.

Greider, William. *One World, Ready or Not: The Manic Logic of Capitalism.* Simon & Shuster, New York, 1997.

Korten, David. *When Corporations Rule the World.* Kumarian Press, San Francisco, 1995.

6-b. New World Government

For most people, the United Nations was supposed to be a kind of global parliament where laws could be made by representatives of all nations to govern the common affairs of the planet. But the power of the UN today has been far outstripped by other international economic institutions, notably the World Trade Organization (WTO), along with the World Bank and the International Monetary Fund. Over the past five years, the WTO has emerged as a major counterweight to the UN in terms of global governance. Yet until the Battle of Seattle, very few people knew anything about the WTO.

From the outset, the WTO was crafted like no other international institution. During the final stages of the GATT negotiations on global trade in 1994, the world's major economic powers (i.e., not only the U.S., Europe, and Japan, but also Canada and leading transnational corporations) wanted to put in place a political organization with the clout required to oversee the building of the global economy. The proposed WTO would be granted both administrative and enforcement powers to ensure that governments adhere to global trade and investment rules designed to advance the interests of transnational corporations and business. By

1995, the adoption of the WTO was railroaded through the legislatures of most countries (including Canada) with little or no public discussion, let alone debate.

Technically, the WTO administers and enforces a body of rules governing the global economy, which include: the General Agreement on Tariffs and Trade; the General Agreement on Trade in Agriculture; and the General Agreement on Trade in Services, plus a series of corresponding rules and disciplines like Trade Related Investment Measures, Trade Related Intellectual Property Rights, Technical Barriers to Trade, and Sanitary and Phyto-Sanitary Measures. While all this may sound like a lot of trade jargon and mumbo-jumbo, the fact is that these global economic rules affect the lives and livelihood of peoples all over the planet.

To administer and enforce these rules, the WTO has been given extraordinary judicial and legislative powers. Under the dispute settlement mechanism of the WTO, member countries, acting on behalf of their own corporate clients, can challenge the laws, policies, and programs of another country as violations of the WTO rules. Panels of unelected experts have the power to adjudicate claims of

Quick Facts:

▶ *Although official WTO decisions are made by votes or consensus in the 140-member General Council, it appears that real decision-making power is now increasingly being exercised through what has become known as the QUAD, namely, the U.S., the European Union, Japan, and Canada. The QUAD convenes separately several times a year between General Council meetings, repeatedly making key decisions on what the WTO will do on major agenda priorities. These QUAD meetings take place behind closed doors, without the participation of other member countries.*

▶ *This WTO governance structure, in turn, is interlocked with, and fortified by, a battery of big business coalitions composed of the most powerful global corporations. This should come as no surprise, since most of world's top global corporations are based in the QUAD countries themselves. According to 1998 rankings, 443 of the Global Fortune 500 corporations are still home-based in either the U.S. (185), Europe (158), or Japan (100). Moreover, big business coalitions like the International Chamber of Commerce (until recently chaired by the CEO of the Nestlé Corporation) function as the general watchdog with direct access to the highest decision-makers in the WTO.*

▶ *In many cases, the WTO rules have actually been directly written by global corporations themselves. Take, for example, the WTO Agreement on Trade Related Intellectual Property Rights (TRIPs). During the Uruguay Round of the GATT negotiations, several leading U.S. corporations—including Bristol Myers Squibb, Dupont, Pfizer, Monsanto, and General Motors—constituted themselves as the Intellectual Property Rights Committee (IPC). In effect, the IPC drafted (almost word for word) the TRIPs Agreement adopted later by the WTO which calls on all countries to incorporate U.S.-style laws protecting 'intellectual property rights' of industrial and pharmaceutical corporations (e.g., granting monopoly sales rights to patent holders for extended periods of time).*

▶ *Several of Canada's own laws and programs are in the process of either being rewritten or struck down as a result of recent WTO rulings. These include: cultural policies requiring Canadian content in foreign magazines sold in Canada; agricultural marketing boards designed to ensure equitable returns for both farmers and consumers in this country; industrial policies providing support for Canadian high-tech industries; major segments of the Auto Pact which has been the centrepiece of Canada' industrial economy for the past half century; plus certain patent laws allowing Canada's generic drug industry to provide drugs at cheaper costs than the pharmaceutical giants claiming protection for their "intellectual property rights."*

▶ *The WTO has launched a new set of negotiations on global trade in agriculture and services, expected to be completed by 2003. Through these negotiations, global rules will be established which will, in effect, increase the powers of transnational corporations over national governments when it comes to the provision of food security and food safety, or public services like health care, education, social, cultural and environmental services. Canada's position in these negotiations is being developed by the Department of International Trade and Foreign Affairs (DFAIT), in collaboration with major Canadian corporations and industries.*

alleged violation of WTO rules and hand out punishments through various kinds of economic sanctions. There are no conflict of interest rules. What's more, they operate in secret, with all documents, hearings and briefs kept confidential.

In turn, these WTO tribunals have the authority, in effect, to strike down domestic laws, policies, and programs of member states judged to be in violation of WTO rules, and/or establish new laws, policies, or programs in conformity with the WTO rules. The panellists have little or no concern for the domestic laws of other countries, let alone respect for the social obligations of governments towards their citizens. As a result, virtually every environmental and health law that has been adjudicated by these WTO tribunals has been declared illegal and ruled "out of order."

Resistance/Activities:

The Battle of Seattle marked the beginning, not the end, of a resistance movement against the WTO as a new World Government. In March 2000, civil society organizations from around the world met to hammer out a plan of action for continuing to fan the flames of the crisis of legitimacy suffered by the WTO and working to curtail its powers. Here in Canada, a coalition of organizations called the Common Front on the WTO has launched a campaign to challenge Ottawa's position in the current WTO negotiations on services affecting public health care, education, water, social security, energy, and environmental services.

In the meantime, youth activists were at the centre of the mass resistance mobilized against the Free Trade Area of the Americas in Quebec City in April 2001. Between 65 and 80 thousand people participated in the week of protest activities that included a People's Summit, a teach-in, marches and demonstrations, plus direct action resistance against the chain-linked wall that had been erected to shield the political leaders and corporate executives involved in the Summit talks.

In preparation for Quebec City, hundreds of young people participated in direct action training camps in Toronto, Ottawa, Halifax and Vancouver.

With remote and inaccessible Qatar hosting the next WTO Ministerial Meeting, resistance is likely to be organized on a more decentralized basis through a pluralism of protest activities in the capitals of WTO member countries, as well as in many local communities.

While the WTO cannot directly command a nation state to change its laws, the threat of economic sanctions creates, if nothing else, a 'chill effect' compelling governments to comply with the WTO rulings.

For all intents and purposes, the WTO has *de facto* become a new world government. Yet citizens have little or no direct access to—let alone participation in—this global governing body. To a large extent, the WTO is run by unelected trade officials working in collaboration with representatives of global corporations. As a result, the WTO poses a major threat to democracy throughout the world.

Discussion Starters:

1. Were you aware of the WTO before? Did you know that the WTO has the judicial and legislative powers to strike down the laws, policies, and programs of democratically elected legislatures? What impact does this have on democracy at home and around the world?

2. What concerns should youth have about the current set of negotiations to establish global rules on what future governments can and cannot do with regard to issues like food safety, health care, public and post-secondary education, social and environmental services? What roles and strategies need to be developed by concerned youth activists?

3. Do we need institutions to govern the global economy? If so, what kinds of institutions and rules need to be developed in the future? What can be done to encourage young people to discuss and debate these issues?

Resource Materials:

Barlow, Maude, and Tony Clarke. *Global Showdown: How the New Activists Are Fighting Global Corporate Rule.* Stoddart, Toronto, 2001.

Clarke, Tony. *By What Authority? Unmasking and Challenging the Global Corporations' Assault on Democracy through the World Trade Organization.* Polaris Institute and the International Forum on Globalization, Ottawa, 1999.

Khor, Martin. "The WTO's Implications for the South," *Third World Resurgence.*

Khor, Martin, Walden Bello, Vandana Shiva, Dot Keet, Sara Larrain and Oronto Douglas. *Views from the South: The Effects of Globalization and the WTO on Third World Countries.* International Forum on Globalization, San Francisco, 2000.

Lee, Marc. *Inside the Fortress: What's Going On at the FTAA Negotiations.* Canadian Centre for Policy Alternatives, Ottawa, 2001.

Nader, Ralph, and Lori Wallach. "GATT, NAFTA, and the Subversion of the Democratic Process," in J. Mander and E. Goldsmith's *The Case Against the Global Economy.* Sierra Club, San Francisco, 1996.

Sinclair, Scott. *GATS: How the World Trade Organization's New "Services" Negotiations Threaten Democracy.* Canadian Centre for Policy Alternatives, Ottawa, 2000.

Shrybman, Steven. *A Citizen's Guide to the World Trade Organization.* Canadian Centre for Policy Alternatives and James Lorimer & Co., Ottawa, 1999.

Wallach, Lori, and Michelle Sforza. *Whose World Trade Organization? Corporate Globalization and the Erosion of Democracy.* Public Citizen Foundation, Washington DC, 1999.

6-c. Global Casino

The fuel that fans the flames of global corporate expansion these days comes from "hot" money generated by a highly combustible mixture of unregulated financial markets and electronic cash flows.

Following the stock market crash of 1929 and the Great Depression, some measures were taken to regulate financial transactions. Commercial banks were required to adhere to rules on reserve requirements, deposit insurance, and limits on interest rate charges. Restrictions were placed on the role of foreign banks, and there was to be a separation between commercial and investment banking. By the 1980s, the big commercial banks around the world had saturated their own national markets and began to demand an opening up of the international financial system through deregulation.

Simultaneously, revolutionary developments in communications technology led to the creation of electronic cash flows, or cyber-money. With one keystroke, currency speculators could move vast sums of money instantaneously around the world. Suddenly, all forms of money could be traded on a 24-hour basis, due to new software used for electronic financial marketing. Moreover, a multi-million-dollar transfer across the world could be completed for a mere 18 cents.

In effect, world financial markets have been transformed into a global financial casino. Through instantaneous electronic transfers, money not only becomes a global product. It also loses its linkages to former sources of value, such as the commodities produced or the services delivered in a community. As a result, the emphasis is on speculative rather than productive forms of investment.

The global banking industry is the main source of financial flows. In 1997, the combined assets of the world's largest 100 banks totalled US $21.3 trillion. This represents an estimated 73% of worldwide economic activity. Throughout the 1990s, overseas investments through pension and mutual funds has skyrocketed, thereby further fuelling the explosion of private financial flows.

It was the creation of this global casino, more than anything else, that was the root cause of the recent Asian financial crisis. The financial melt-down that began in Thailand in 1997 and spread like wildfire through Malaysia, the Philippines, and South Korea was primarily provoked by investors speculating on 'hot' currencies and commodities in order to make a fast profit.

Commercial banks, investment houses, and brokerage firms in the U.S. and other industrialized countries served as the vehicles for this speculation. When prices began to tumble and speculators en masse pulled out their investments, the economies of these countries started to crumble. At this point, the commercial banks, investment houses, and brokerage firms became creditors demanding bailout money for their loans. Working hand-in-glove with the International Monetary Fund and the central banks of the industrialized countries (e.g., the U.S. Treasury and the Bank of Canada, etc.) a $121 billion package was arranged, most of which went to 're-pay' the financial institutions that were responsible for the speculative assault in the first place.

Quick Facts:

▶ As much as US $2 trillion is circulated around the globe on a daily basis, which in turn amounts to 60 times the volume of goods and services that are traded each day in world markets.

▶ Electronic transfer systems like CHIPS, a New York bank clearing house, makes more than 150,000 international money transactions in a single day, at such a speed and frequency that it is virtually impossible to trace, let alone regulate.

▶ The Bank for International Settlements estimates that present telecommunications technology and systems could handle as much as US $13 trillion in financial transactions around the world on a daily basis.

▶ Increasingly, corporations are rapidly becoming financial institutions in their own right, even to the point where they are replacing big commercial banks as major players. General Electric, for example, is now recognized as one of the largest financial institutions in the world.

▶ The power which the global financial casino puts in the hands of currency traders is awesome, when one considers that the average daily transaction of US $1.3 trillion far exceeds the combined resources available to the central banks of national governments around the world, which is estimated to be US $640 billion.

▶ The power which individual speculators have over nation states was dramatically illustrated in 1992 when financier George Soros, in order to win a bet with British Prime Minister John Major, sold $10 billion worth of sterling on world financial markets for a $1 billion profit, thereby forcing a devaluation of the British pound and the break-up of the new exchange rates system that the European Union was planning to instate.

▶ Currency speculators already play a major role in determining a broad spectrum of national government policies, ranging from credit systems, money supply, and interest rates to debt management, investment policies, and taxation. In effect, the managers of "hot" money have emerged as a "disciplinary" force in global markets, compelling national governments to adopt stiff austerity measures when they want them to. As one New York banker put it: "Countries don't control their own destiny. If they don't discipline themselves, the world market will do it for them."

Resistance/Activities:

The World Bank and the IMF have been the prime targets of popular resistance against the global financial casino. When these financial institutions held their annual meetings in Washington, DC, in April 2000, tens of thousands of people, led by youth activists, mobilized for A-16 through a series of teach-ins, marches, and direct action. Six months later, similar forms of resistance were mounted in Prague when the IMF and World Bank meetings were held there in September 2000.

These mobilizations of resistance have been fortified by policy analysis provided by groups like 50 Years Is Enough in the U.S. and the Halifax Initiative in Canada. Moreover, a proposed set of IMF-World Bank meetings scheduled for Barcelona in June 2001 were cancelled when it became known that mass protests were planned.

Resource Materials:

Barnet, Richard and John Cavanagh, "Electronic Money and the Casino Economy," *The Case Against the Global Economy.* Jerry Mander & Edward Goldsmith eds. Sierra Club Books, 1996.

Bello, Walden. "The Malaysian Enigma" and a series of related articles on the Asian financial crisis, *Focus on Trade*, Bangkok: Focus on the Global South, www.focusweb.org

Chossudovsky, Michel. "The G-7 Solution to the Global Financial Crisis: A Marshall Plan for Creditors and Speculators." Ottawa: distributed by e-mail by author at chossudovsky@sprint.ca

Dillon, John. *Turning the Tide: Confronting the Money Traders.* Canadian Centre for Policy Alternatives Publication, Ottawa, 1996.

Greider, William. *One World, Ready or Not: The Manic Logic of Global Capitalism.* Simon & Shuster, New York, 1997.

Korten, David. *The Post-Corporate World: Life After Capitalism.* Berrett- Koehler Publishers and Kumarian Press, San Francisco, 1999.

See also, *Economic Justice Report: A Periodical on Global Issues of Economic Justice.* Contains regular articles on Canada and the global financial crisis. Available on order from the Ecumenical Coalition for Economic Justice, 947 Queen Street East, Suite 208, Toronto, Ontario Canada M4M 1J9. Email: ecej@accessv.com

Discussion Starters:

1. What does this say about the power wielded by money traders and commercial banks today? What happens when national governments surrender their sovereign rights to regulate the inflows and outflows of capital?

2. What concerns should youth today have about a casino economy built on speculative rather than productive investment? Can you cite some examples of increasing speculative investment in Canada or elsewhere? What about your own community? What happens when our commercial banks cater to global markets rather than community needs in their loans?

3. What are the dangers of foreign investors taking a speculative run on the Canadian dollar? What steps could be taken by Ottawa to control foreign speculative investment? What about putting a financial transactions tax on all such transactions as a means of curbing speculative investments? What could be done to begin mobilizing public support for these ideas?

4. What could be done to institute the proposed Tobin Tax (named after Nobel Prize-winning economist James Tobin) that would put a levy on all global financial transactions, which in turn would create a large pool of capital that could be used to meet the basic needs of people and the planet, especially in the Third World?

6-d. Militarism

The Cold War between the United States and the Soviet Union that dominated global politics for most of the 20th century may be over, but the military arms race that fuelled it is far from over. On the contrary, there has been no substantial decrease in world military expenditures since the end of the Cold War. Every year, $780 billion is still spent on military weapons and operations around the world.

The global economy, in other words, remains highly militarized. At its core lies the aerospace and defence industry. It is comprised of some of the largest transnational corporations in the world, such as Lockheed Martin, Daimler Chrysler Aerospace, Boeing, Aerospatial, and British Aerospace. While most of these corporations are known for their aircraft production, they also produce weapons for military customers. The industry, of course, is primarily based in the technologically advanced regions of the U.S. and Europe. Yet, its major market in this post-Cold War era has been developing countries in the South.

Today, access to advanced aerospace capability provides governments and nation states with international prestige and power. The aerospace and defence industry is able to deliver technologically advanced fight-

ers, bombers, missiles, and related weapon systems to any country in demand. As well, a substantial portion of the annual budgets of national governments is earmarked either for direct military spending or for aerospace industry subsidies (e.g., R&D grants, export financing, tax credits, etc.). Through this system, the northern industrialized countries where the industry is based are not only able to manufacture weapons for export to many southern developing countries, but they also strengthen their technological capability by doing so.

Unlike any other industry, however, military production enjoys blanket protection in the global economy through international trade and investment agreements. Virtually all modern trade agreements and institutions like the World Trade Organization contain an operating clause which exempts all government programs and policies deemed necessary for national security from the application of trade rules and disciplines. Article 21 of the GATT, for example, spells out this 'national security exemption' for the WTO (see 'Quick Facts'). What this means, in effect, is that one area of the global economy where governments are given a free rein to spend public revenues is in the field of military production and operations.

In turn, this 'national security exemption' serves to increase military spending and production. This became clear when a WTO dispute panel ruled against Canada's Technology Partnerships program for providing subsidies to the Bombardier Aerospace company to build and export regional passenger jets. Government subsidies for non-military production were considered illegal under the WTO rules. But, when Ottawa redesigned its Technology Partnerships program to provide subsidies to Bombardier for the development of new weapons, the program was declared WTO-friendly because it fell within the "national security exemption."

For youth today, this re-militarization of the global economy provides shaky grounds on which build a world without war in the 21st century.

Quick Facts:

► *According to the World Game Institute in the U.S., global military expenditures amount to $780 billion on an annual basis. By contrast, the Institute estimates that $237.5 billion is spent each year on global programs for addressing major human needs and environmental problems. The combined cost of these programs is 30% of the world's total annual expenditures.*

► *Over a decade after the end of the Cold War, the U.S. maintains some 2,500 missile-mounted nuclear warheads on 'hair-trigger alert,' while Russia has some 2,000 nuclear warheads on similar high alert. Recent plans by the U.S. to authorize the redeployment of the Star Wars program of building a nuclear defence shield could accelerate nuclear weapons production again, thereby destroying the Anti-Ballistic Missile Treaty.*

► *Canada has the fourth largest aerospace and defence industry in the world, following the United States, the United Kingdom, and France. Unlike the other leading countries in this field, Canada's industry has a high degree of foreign ownership. With some 42% of industry revenues in Canada going to U.S.-based corporations, the Canadian aerospace and defence industry is largely an extension of the American military economy.*

► *The 'security exemption' clause in Article 21 of the GATT and the WTO states that a country cannot be stopped from taking whatever action it deems necessary to protect its essential security interests—actions "relating to the traffic in arms, ammunition, and implements of war, and such traffic in other goods and materials as is carried on directly for the purpose of supplying a military establishment [or] taken in time of war or other emergency in international relations."*

Discussion Starters:

1. Did the end of the Cold War mean the end of militarization? What are the links between economic globalization and militarism?

2. What are the implications of the "security exemption" clause in the General Agreement on Trade and Tariffs (Article 21 of the GATT)? Whose interests does this clause serve? How does the clause reinforce the links between militarism and global trade?

3. To what extent are today's youth concerned about an increasingly militarized global economy? What can be done to stimulate discussion and debate about these issues in the classroom, on campuses, and in the workplace?

Resource Materials:

"The Corporate War Machine," a series of articles published by *Multinational Monitor*, March 1998. Available online at www.essential.org/monitor

Press for Conversion. quarterly journal of the Coalition to Oppose the Arms Trade (COAT). (See website at www.ncf.ca/coat/)

Project Ploughshares, Monitor. A monthly publication on issues of Canadian military production. Available from Project Ploughshares website: www.ploughshares.ca

Public Education for Peace Society. A Series of six *fact-sheets* on militarism and globalization, available from End the Arms Race, 405-825 Granville Street, Vancouver B.C. V6Z-1K9.

Staples, Steven. *Confronting the Military-Corporate Complex.* presentation to the Hague Appeal for Peace. Available from End the Arms Race website: www.peacewire.org

6-e. Human Rights

One of the ongoing critical issues of concern to many youth around the world today is the continuous repression of human rights that takes place in various countries. All too often, the militarized governments in these countries operate hand-in-glove with foreign-based corporations which have come to access their valuable resources or exploit their cheap labour. When this happens, state repression of human rights is fortified.

A prime example has been in Nigeria, where Shell Oil is known to have paid the security forces of the Nigerian military for protection against social unrest by the Ogoni people. Since 1958, Shell has established major operations in the rich lands of the Ogoni, drilling over 100 wells and setting up two refineries. Despite constant promises of a better life, the Ogoni region remains deeply impoverished, with dilapidated hospitals and schools, while Shell Oil and other petroleum giants continue to plunder the resource, extracting millions upon millions of dollars of oil at great ecological as well as economic expense to the indigenous people.

Not far away, in Sudan, Canadian oil companies are working with the Sudanese military government, which has been repeatedly condemned by the United Nations for its brutal repression of human rights, including the practice of slavery. For the past 16 years, a savage civil war has been waged in Sudan, claiming over two million lives, mainly civilians. Since 1997, Calgary-based Talisman Energy, Canada's largest independent petroleum producer, has led a consortium of oil producers in the development of the Greater Nile Oil Project and the construction of a mega-pipeline. Since these oil developments lie at the heart of the current conflict, the Sudanese military provides Talisman and other foreign-based companies with thousands of armed troops for 'protection.' As a result, Talisman is simply aiding and abetting the systematic repression of human rights in Sudan.

Indeed, corporate-sponsored repression of human rights is taking place all over the world. Take Pepsi-Cola's steadfast support for the brutal military dictatorship in Burma, or the Freeport mining giant's solid backing of the Suharto regime in Indonesia which was responsible for the murder of some two million people in East Timor alone. And then there's the scourge of child labour and sweatshop practices by brand-name corporations, ranging from the giant retailer Wal-Mart to the mighty footwear manufacturer Nike and the entertainment colossus Disney.

Quick Facts:
(on Talisman and the Human Rights in Sudan)

▶ *The consortium of oil producers led by Talisman in Sudan includes companies from China, Malaysia, and the Sudan. Drilling from existing wells in the Greater Nile Oil Project began in 1998, followed by the establishment of processing plans and the construction of the pipeline. By the summer of 1999, oil was flowing through the pipeline to Port Sudan for export. With goals of producing 150,000 barrels a day, Talisman provides oil free of charge to the Sudanese government, thereby allowing other revenues to be used to finance the civil war.*

▶ *In response to constant pressure from Canadian church and human rights groups, Ottawa opened talks with Talisman officials to stop fuelling the civil war. When the talks proved to be futile, Ottawa warned the company that it could face sanctions if it did not mend its ways. The Government also appointed former international labour official John Harker to conduct a special fact-finding visit to investigate human rights violations in Sudan. Beyond these moves, however, no effective action has been taken to rein in Talisman and its operations in Sudan.*

▶ *According to the Harker report, the Sudanese military has been making use of the roads and airstrip constructed by Talisman and the consortium for its military operations. The roads have "enabled troops to reach their destination more easily than before. Flights clearly linked to the oil war," says the Harker report, "have been a regular feature of life at the Heglig airstrip, which is adjacent to the oil workers' compound...Canadian chartered helicopters and fixed wing aircraft which use the strip have shared the facilities with helicopter gunships and Antonov bombers of the GOS. These have armed and refuelled at Helgig and from there attacked civilians.*

▶ *The Harker report concludes "that oil is exacerbating conflict in Sudan." The drive "to exploit oil deposits...which can only be done with foreign help, has intensified the conflict in four ways": first, concern about oilfield security has brought displacement, pacification and insecurity to the region; second, it has accelerated the fighting, not only between the military and the rebels, but also people in the oil regions; third, it has increased the military's war-fighting capacity by providing them with airstrips and roads; fourth, it has elevated concern about control over natural resources and the southern region of the country.*

▶ *While many more cases could be cited, we should also remember there are signs of hope, as well. It was a youth-led rebellion in Indonesia that forced Suharto to eventually resign, leading to the release of thousands of human rights activists from prison, including labour leader Muchtar Pakpahan.*

Discussion Starters:

1. What role do transnational corporations play in the violation of human rights in other countries? How can foreign investment or the operations of foreign-based corporations be used to strengthen the hand of oppression by the state?

2. Should the Canadian government exercise responsibility for monitoring and regulating the operations of Canadian-based corporations like Talisman in other countries?

3. What actions can be taken to ensure that Canadian-based corporations do not, directly or indirectly, help foreign governments to oppress their own citizens? What kinds of legislative initiatives and legal actions could be undertaken? What can be done to raise public awareness about these corporate or corporate-assisted violations of human rights—in your classroom, campus, or workplace?

Resource Materials:

Harker, John. *Human Security in Sudan: The Report of a Canadian Assessment Mission.* Prepared for Foreign Affairs. Ottawa, January 2000.

Interchurch Committee on Africa. *Cries From The Heart.* A report on human rights violations in the Sudan. 1999.

Kretzmann, Steve. "Nigeria's Drilling Fields," *Multinational Monitor.* A special edition on "Multinationals and Hunman Rights," vol. 16, no. 1-2, Jan.-Feb., 1995.

Weisman, Robert. "Stolen Youth: Brutalized Children, Globalization and the Campaign to End Child Labour," *Multinational Monitor*, vol. 18, no. 1-2, Jan.-Feb., 1997.

PART IV

Methods
&
Tools

ORGANIZING TIPS

Learning to live and act in McWorld is no easy feat. If this is the first generation to "grow up corporate," then it is important that concerned youth have the opportunity to develop the methods, tools, and skills required to face-up to the challenges of McWorld and to fight for democracy and the commons.

The time has come to dig in for the long haul. To do so, youth activists will need to develop their own capacities for taking control over their economic, social, and ecological future. This means developing the kinds of skills and tools required to effectively challenge corporate rule in its diverse manifestations.

The starting points for many young activists lie in our universities and schools, our workplaces and our communities. The leadership capacities acquired in these settings will enable youth activists to go on and take up some of the major issues and challenges of corporate power that lie behind the problems of economic, social,

and ecological insecurity that plague the majority of people in Canada and the world at large.

Developing these kinds of capacities will, however, require some new skills and tools. Most of the conventional methods for bringing about democratic social change in this country have been designed to reform or transform the policies and practices of governments alone. Little has been done to design skills and tools to challenge and transform the operations of corporations as political machines that are controlling what governments can and cannot do, let alone the capitalist system itself.

It is, therefore, important to focus attention here on identifying what kinds of methods and resources—research, education, organizing, campaigns, alternatives, coalitions—are necessary for tackling the corporate power structures that are the driving forces behind what governments and related institutions are doing today.

A. Challenging McWorld

In order to build youth capacities for challenging McWorld, it is important to first come to grips with the culture of resistance that is emerging in this age of corporate globalization. In some countries, the kind of resistance that has been mounting is not only political and economic, but also cultural and localized at the same time.

Take, for example, the gathering of over 100,000 people that took place in Millau, France, over a June 2000 weekend. The occasion was not another meeting of global leaders like the WTO or the IMF. Instead, it was the trial of José Bové and the McDo 10. When the WTO ruled against the European ban on hormone-treated beef, allowing the U.S., Canada, and other beef-exporting countries to raise tariffs on their imports of European products as a penalty, one of the targets was the world-famous Roquefort cheese which is made from sheep's milk in the farming communities around Millau.

Protesting against the WTO ruling, José Bové and nine other small farmers decided to smash the construction of a local McDonalds' franchise as a global symbol of their resistance.

So what McDonald's officials publicly labelled as a "wrecking party," the local farmers called a "festival of destruction." Of the 100,000 who gathered in Millau, however, approximately 35,000 reportedly came to witness the trial, while the remaining 65,000 or so showed up for a rock concert that weekend. Yet the two events were closely related. The rock band's concert in Millau was organized in support of the McDo 10. What's more, thousands joined in the chant, "The World Is Not For Sale And Neither Am I," which just happens to be the title of Bové's recent book. And, to top it all off, political cartoonists throughout Europe had a field day, drawing José Bové's handlebar moustache in the shape of McDonald's golden arches logo.

Underlying the McDo 10 trial, however, is the fact that dissent itself is once again being targeted as a criminalized activity. During the WTO protests in Seattle, the Pentagon's top secret Delta Force, which was featured in the Waco standoff, had established its own command post in a downtown hotel. At the A-16 demonstrations in Washington, D.C., undercover police were deployed everywhere and phones were tapped to monitor 73 Internet sites of campaign activists.

In a RAND study prepared for the Pentagon, civil society activists against corporate globalization are portrayed as an "NGO swarm" that can "sting a victim to death" through Internet action. To stir up conflict between civil society groups, the Pentagon has reportedly begun to ignite what it calls "social net wars" amongst groups over controversial issues. And, here in Canada, a report by CSIS (the Canadian Security Intelligence Service) describes the critics of unregulated capitalism as "militant anarchists."

All of this points to the need to deepen our understanding of resistance in an age of corporate globalization. Ursula Franklin, professor emeritus at the University of Toronto and one of this country's long-standing environmental and peace activists, maintains that the time has come for people to recognize that we are living under conditions of military occupation, where the corporations are the new armies of occupation, and there is much to learn from the French Resistance Movement. The end of the Cold War, she says, did not mean the end of war-making. Military tactics have simply shifted to the economic arena, and what we now have is an economic war being waged against people.

The new enemy, she contends, is 'the people,' and the new territories of occupation are 'the commons,' such as health care, education, culture, the environment, and all the other elements of common life that used to be protected and enhanced by the public sector. What we have now, with this new style of military occupation, Prof. Franklin argues, is "puppet governments...running the country on behalf of corporations and their armies of marketeers."

Like the French resistance, says Franklin, we too find ourselves acting as "collaborators with the armies of occupation." After all, the places where we work, buy products and services, and secure the food we eat are very often connected, one way or another, to the corporations which are the armies of occupation. In order to protect our families and survive, we collaborate with our occupiers in various ways. But we can also develop strategies and tactics of resistance in order to block their advance wherever possible.

Unlike the Nazi occupiers of Europe, today's corporate occupiers do not wear uniforms. So we must learn to identify, unmask, and expose them and their operations wherever we can. This is the kind of discipline that needs to be developed if we are to deepen and broaden the resistance for the long run as a stepping stone to building a post-corporate society.

B. Corporate Analysis

In order to build a culture of resistance to McWorld and its underlying forces, it is important for youth activists to develop and strengthen their capacities for corporate analysis. After all, McWorld symbolizes a new political era in which the transnational corporation has become the dominant institution of our times. As we have seen, 52 of the top 100 economies in the world today are transnational corporations. Wal-Mart's annual revenues are larger than those of 163 individual nation states on this planet. General Motors has a larger economy than either Hong Kong, Denmark, or Thailand. Ford Motor Co.'s sales are bigger than South Africa's GDP, Shell outstrips oil-rich Saudi Arabia, while Japan's Itochu Co. has a higher GDP than countries like Greece, Finland, Malaysia, Portugal or Israel. And cigarette-peddler Philip Morris enjoys annual sales that are greater than the GDPs of 148 countries.

Simply put, transnational corporations dominate virtually every facet of our daily lives. Just take the youth-related issues and struggles we have been discussing in this book. Whether we are talking about campus issues like the debt wall or commercialized research; high school issues like business-school partnerships or consumer youth marketing; workplace issues like contingent work or the health and safety rights of young workers; national policy issues like genetically engineered foods or climate change and global warming; or international policy concerns related to the World Trade Organization or the World Bank and the International Monetary Fund—you can be sure that transnational corporations and financial institutions are at the centre of these diverse battlefronts. Along with governments, therefore, it is crucial that we make those corporations and industries, the dominant players behind these various struggles, the major targets of our actions for resistance and change.

In developing campaign strategies for confronting McWorld, it is equally important to recognize that we are dealing with corporate-dominated governments. In this age of economic globalization, the role and powers of the state have been radically altered to primarily serve the interests of transnational capital, not the needs and rights of its citizens.

Here in Canada, we have seen the emergence of a corporate-government regime as the BCNI and its 150 member corporations have increasingly gained a stranglehold on Ottawa's policy-making apparatus. Fortified by corporate "think tanks" *like the C.D. Howe and Fraser institutes, and citizen front groups like the National Citizens' Coalition and the Canadian Taxpayers' Association, the BCNI and its member corporations have effectively waged a series of assaults on the provision of universal social programs and public services in this country, through its relentless campaigns for deregulation and privatization, tax cuts, and free trade.*

Confronting McWorld, therefore, means taking on the corporate/government regimes that now determine (if not dictate) peoples' daily lives. To do so, the corporate power that lies behind these regimes needs to be identified, unmasked, and targeted for action. Whatever issues and policy struggles become the focal point of youth-based campaigns, there will be a need to develop the skills and tools to analyze the corporate players involved.

*One way of doing so is to do an x-ray of the corporation and its industry. This method involves dissecting the component parts or operations of a corporation in the context of its industry, and assessing its strengths and weaknesses for the strategic purpose of organizing an effective campaign. Conducting these x-rays requires developing a set of pro-*files of the corporations targeted for campaign action. These profiles are meant to provide x-ray charts disclosing strategic intelligence and information that may be useful in developing corporate campaigns.

These corporate x-rays involve five profiles: an organizational profile of the company's management, charter, legal and organizational structure in the industry; an economic profile of research, production, marketing, and financial operations of the corporation and the industry; a political profile of the company's public policy positions, government lobbying, public relations, and international operations; a social profile of the corporation's track record and performance regarding labour, community, social, environmental, and health issues; and a stakeholder profile of the major players in the corporation and the industry (i.e., investors, customers, suppliers, workers, creditors, and community). In conducting these x-ray profiles, priority is put on assessing what the corporation's strengths and weaknesses are as a potential target for mounting a campaign of resistance and transformation. Much of the information required for these corporate x-rays is already available online.

In effect, this is the method used by veteran labour organizer Ray Rogers, founder of Corporate Campaigns in the U.S. Before starting any campaign, Rogers insists on doing a "power analysis" of the major players. Doing homework, for example, on the CEO, board of directors, and top management of the corporation(s) and industry involved in a particular set of issues, he says, "I research them thoroughly so that I understand how much influence they really wield in terms of the other institutions they're tied into, their political connections, etc. Then I lay everything out on a chart. And I begin to get a picture of who really wields power." Once this is done, he says, the leverage points for exerting change and countervailing pressures can be identified.

Then "the next step is to identify the power that can carry out the plan. The (alternative countervailing) power is based on people and money. Who can be mobilized?" Are there allied unions and community groups who have significant bank accounts and insurance policies that can be called upon to withdraw and/or reinvest their money? Are there allied organizations that do business with the suppliers and customers of the targeted corporation, and which can, in turn, exert pressure?

C. Network Organizing

The use of the Internet by youth activists has already revolutionized political organizing. As an organizing tool, the Internet creates a flat structure of communication across the board. Through the Net, people everywhere can have direct access to a culture of instant information swapping. Thousands of people can be mobilized to take part in a public event, with little in the way of bureaucracy. Online, individuals can pick and choose where and when to plug-in. Once connected, no one is compelled to give up their individuality. Everyone is free to dip-in, dip-out, or delete. As Naomi Klein notes, "It is a surfer's approach to activism."

What has been particularly innovative, however, is the way the Net has been used by youth activists as an organizing tool for collective goals and purposes.

Take movements like Reclaim The Streets (RTS), which originated in the United Kingdom. As a form of urban environmentalism, RTS has been organizing street parties in major city centres since 1995 for the main purpose, as coordinator John Jordan describes it, "of reclaiming space for collective use— as commons." Each party is locally organized, drawing thousands of mainly youth to reclaim the communal space of the streets, combining rave and rage through a mixture of dance, music and art. Initially viewed as anti-car protests, RTS activities have expanded to include a much broader critique of society and globalization. In the late 1990s, for example, street parties were organized in support of London Underground workers, Liverpool dock workers, plus ecological and human rights campaigns against Shell, BP and Mobil.

Or take the time that Reclaim the Streets organized the first ever Global Street Party. The idea was to create some common public space in several major cities to highlight issues of corporate globalization at the time of the G-8 leaders' summit in Birmingham in May, 1998. When the idea was floated on e-mail, groups in some 30 cities around the world took up the challenge. In Utrecht, the Netherlands, 800 people blocked a six-lane highway and danced for five hours. In Berlin, a thousand more people held a rave in a downtown intersection, while in Sydney, Australia, some 3,500 activists "kidnapped" a road and staged three live concerts with bands. Each RTS event was organized by a local organization—the hub—involving dozens of other "spoke-groups."

At the same time, the Direct Action Network and the Ruckus Society in the U.S. have been primarily responsible for training youth activists in civil disobedience, dramatic stunts, and affinity groups. In particular, these two youth-led initiatives made their mark on the style of organizing and training for direct action that characterized the battles of Seattle, Washington, and Prague. A similar training approach was used by transAction in Toronto to prepare some 400 youth activists for the mobilization in Quebec City.

The new organizing developments also include more internationalized forms of civil society networks. For example, Peoples' Global Action (PGA) has developed a style of organizing which mobilizes a worldwide network of youth activists around the major meetings of the global governors. When the G-8 leaders met in Cologne in June, 1999, for example, the

PGA played a key organizing role on at least two fronts: co-sponsoring with RST and other groups a "global carnival against capital" which targeted the role and power of transnational corporations in the global economy; and facilitating an intercontinental caravan of 500 Indian farmers travelling across western Europe, which included protest stops at the country headquarters of Cargill, Monsanto, and other agribusiness giants.

Web organizing has also been effectively used by resistance movements like ATTAC and Jubilee 2000. ATTAC, initially organized in France, has become the base for a series of European campaigns on a range of globalization issues such as the elimination of tax havens, the restructuring of the WTO, the promotion of the Tobin Tax on speculative financial transactions, and the dismantling of free trade negotiations like the Transatlantic Economic Partnership. And Jubilee 2000 has provided a new vehicle for revitalizing faith communities around the world to become a significant force for the cancellation of Third World debts.

The political effectiveness of Web organizing through the *hub-and-spoke model should also not be underestimated. Since its organizing principles are different from those of its institutional targets, i.e., corporations and governments, it has often proven to be very difficult to control. "It responds to corporate concentration with a maze of fragmentation," says Naomi Klein, "to globalization with its own kind of localization, to power consolidation with radical power dispersal." Groups of activists, who are not tied down with bureaucratic or hierarchical structure, are usually able to make use of these tools to respond quickly by mobilizing large numbers, like a swarm of bees in a surprise attack.*

The RAND corporation used a similar analogy when it described in a study how the Zapatista movement in Chiapas, Mexico, was able to turn a "war of the flea" into a "war of the swarm" by using the Internet in 1994-5 to mobilize support from civil society groups all over the world. For military strategists, said the RAND study, the key problem posed by the "war of the swarm" is that it has no "central leadership or command structure; it is multi-headed, impossible to decapitate. And it can sting a victim to death."

D. Advocacy Networks

While much has been said about the fact that recent mass protests would not have happened without the use of the Internet, Klein reminds us, little attention has been given to how this new communication technology is reshaping the structure of social change movements. Like it or not, today's civil society movements are being shaped in the image of the Net. As we shall see, this has not only many up-sides, but some down-sides as well when it comes to building a new democracy movement

In their recent book, *Globalization From Below*, Jeremy Brecher, Tim Costello, and Brendan Smith contend that the rise of network organizing "reflects the decline in the importance of traditional organization" such as labour unions, community organizations, and political parties. In a time when thousands of people lived in the same neighbourhoods, worked in the same workplaces, and participated in the same culture, it was natural that they shared a common interest nurtured by belonging to the same unions, parties, and other organizations. But in today's world this kind of unity has been broken down by the individualism and fragmentation that characterizes everyday life in a high-tech society. As a form of political organizing, 'advocacy networks' are an attempt to rekindle the kinds of 'collectivity' that may be more viable in an increasingly individualized and fragmented society.

Advocacy networks are generally composed of activists and other people who are committed to work together in building resistance and developing alternatives around a particular set of public policy issues or structural problems in society. In their campaigns, advocacy networks operate differently from either conventional civil society organizations or formal coalitions. While there may be a lead organization for the campaign, or even a coalition of supporters, the planning and organizing is carried out by a network of committed persons. Compared to conventional organizations, advocacy networks require a high level of personal commitment and responsibility. Often working across formal organizational lines, advocacy networks are characterized by what has been called 'cross-organizational team leadership."

In Canada, civil society groups have experimented with advocacy networks as an alternative form of political organizing during the past two decades. The Action Canada Network, for example, which led the fight against both the FTA and NAFTA through national and international campaigns in the late 1980s and early '90s, was an earlier form of advocacy network. In its operations, the ACN was largely composed of committed activists representing a broad spectrum of major labour unions and community organizations which exemplified a kind of cross-organizational team leadership in developing and carrying out campaigns. As the ACN's successor, the Solidarity Network and groups like the Canadian Health Coalition operate along similar lines.

The MAI campaign provided a different model of advocacy networking in that one organization—the Council of Canadians—took the lead in planning and organizing, with buy-ins from other civil society organizations and activists. Similarly, the Ontario Days of Action, which mobilized widespread public opposition to the 'slash and burn' economic agenda of the Mike Harris government, was spearheaded by the Ontario Federation of Labour and its affiliates, with active participation from a broad cross- section of community groups and individual citizens.

A feature of advocacy networks is that they allow for a diversity of participation on the part of groups and individuals from a variety of sectors. Segments of civil society organizations can participate directly in such networks and in the campaigns they launch, while other segments can remain aloof. Individuals, whether they formally belong to a civil society organization or not, can usually participate directly in network planning and organizing activities.

The key factor in determining participation lies in the "framing" of the issues and struggles. As the co-authors of *Globalization From Below* put it, "framing" is a "conscious strategic effort" by the participants of advocacy networks to develop a shared understanding of their struggle to transform the world and themselves which, in turn, serves to "legitimate and motivate collective action." In effect, the "frame" defines the purpose and identity of the network and, to the extent to which individuals accept the frame, determines the degree of active participation.

E. Hub and Spokes

Advocacy networks operate best in terms of the hub-and-spokes model. Naomi Klein's description of the Internet as being "not one giant web but a network of 'hubs and spokes'" provides a useful metaphor for understanding the emerging structure and form of movements for social change. The metaphor itself is based on the insights of TeleGeography, a Washington-based research centre which has mapped out the architecture of the Internet as if it were the solar system. As with the Net, the hubs are the centres of activity, while the spokes, which are both autonomous and interconnected, serve as links to other centres.

Applying this metaphor to interpret the mass protests, Klein says that the convergence centres were the activist hubs which, in turn, were composed of "hundreds, possibly thousands, of autonomous spokes." The spokes themselves were made up of "affinity groups" comprising five to 20 protesters, who in turn elected one person to represent them at regular "spokescouncil meetings." The affinity groups all agreed to adhere to basic principles of nonviolence, but each retained the authority to collectively make its own strategic decisions for action as a group.

By their very nature and structure, advocacy networks are conducive to providing the political space for individual youth activists and their groups to work together as a community. Not only have they demonstrated a capacity to forge cooperation among diverse constituencies, but their fluidity allows them to adapt to today's high velocity of change without losing sight of basic principles. Any attempt to monopolize or block the flow of communication, either within networks or between civil society organizations, is usually strongly resisted.

Advocacy networks also resist dominant leaders, emphasizing styles of leadership based on respect and persuasion, rather than charisma, let alone authoritarianism. When they delegate authority, it is not done on a permanent basis, and is renewable only through active trust. As a result, these kinds of networks are more likely than many conventionally structured civil society organizations to resist takeover by sectarian groups.

But there are also some limitations to these new organizing methods. For example, they can allow some organizations which possess technical expertise, organizational clout, and financial *resources to operate as a new élite. This élitism is as much present in the civil society movement against corporate globalization as it is anywhere else. It often manifests itself in relations between community-based grassroots groups and nationally—or internationally— based organizations involved in policy research and lobbying activities. When the latter dominate the agenda with* their technical expertise and lobbying campaigns, the former frequently end up being systematically shut out of meaningful and effective participation in the movement against corporate globalization. Unless this élitism is checked and rooted out, the potential for building a new democracy movement to transform the global economy will be severely limited.

F. Collective Power

So where do youth activists acquire the "power" to effectively confront McWorld and build a post-corporate society? Well, like all other social movements in a democratic society, the power of youth lies in their capacity to collectively withdraw their consent from those who govern and rule. After all, democratic societies are based on a set of social relationships between the main groups of players—relationships which are sustained through various forms of consent. The balance of power between the main social groupings is maintained through rules and laws that are mutually accepted. When the consent of the people is withdrawn, then the balance of power is disrupted, opening the door for social transformation. Even by threatening to withdraw their *consent, people can collectively exercise power.*

In other words, the power of existing social relations is based on the active cooperation of some people and the consent and/or acquiescence of others. It is the activity of people—going to work, paying taxes, buying products, obeying government officials, staying off private property—that continually recreates the power of the powerful. This dependence gives people a potential power over society—but one that can be realized only if they are prepared to withhold their acquiescence. In response to such threats, the ruling élites will often prefer to make concessions rather than risk having the ultimate source of their power completely undermined.

In his classic three-volume treatise on *The Politics of Non-Violent Action*, Gene Sharpe contends that "the exercise of power depends on the consent of the ruled who, by withdrawing that consent, can control and even destroy the power of their opponent." In nonviolent struggles, however, Sharpe stresses that the aim is not to annihilate the opponent, but to undercut his or her strength in order to force a shift in the balance of power. According to Sharpe, the withdrawal of consent from established power and authority can take many forms. Through case studies, he identifies nearly 200 methods of nonviolent action that have been used by civil society movements in the past to withdraw consent or organize dissent. The most frequent methods used, however, are strikes, boycotts, and civil disobedience.

The collective withdrawal of consent by a significant portion of civil society creates a "crisis of legitimacy" for established institutions in terms of their power and authority. In effect, this is what happened in Seattle where the battle that raged on the streets, coupled with mounting frustration and dissension in the ranks of Third World delegations during the ministerial meetings, provoked a "crisis of legitimacy" around the WTO. Similarly, in India, a "crisis of legitimacy" erupted over the World Bank when a build-up of mass local resistance to the proposed Narmada Dam for its destructive effects on communities and the environment forced the Bank to withdraw its funding.

Earlier, intense opposition by local villagers in India had also compelled DuPont, the global chemical giant, to abandon its plans to build a plant in the region and the central and state governments to withdraw their support for the project. By the same token, the withdrawal of France from the MAI negotiations, triggered in large measure by civil society opposition, led to a collapse of what would have been a global corporate rule treaty, as other governments, including Canada, withdrew their support.

The power of youth to undermine the authority and legitimacy of governments and corporations, however, is largely contingent on the exercise of nonviolent forms of action. It is one thing for nonviolent direct actions, exercised by youth activists, to provoke a violent reaction by the state through the unleashing of police or military forces. But when those factions of the anarchist groups that are committed to violence as a *means for social change go on a rampage to destroy buildings and other property in the streets of Geneva, Seattle, Prague, or Quebec City, they create a "crisis of legitimacy" for the rest of the civil society movement in the minds of the public at large.*

*One can well understand the anger, despair, and even bitterness that youth anarchists feel towards governments and corporations for what they are do-*ing to people and the planet. There are moments in history when people have had no other choice but to use violence as a last resort to prevent total annihilation. But civil society generally loses its own power and authority when violence becomes the means for social change. Morally and politically, it also happens to be the wrong foundation on which to build a new democracy and a post-corporate society.

G. Direct Action

Prior to and beyond the battle of Seattle, youth activists have led the way in reviving the use of nonviolent forms of direct action in struggles for democratic social change. Traditionally, direct action methods like sit-ins, occupations, blockades, and other types of civil disobedience have been important tactical tools for building popular resistance against dominant power structures. Throughout most of the past quarter-century, however, there appears to have been a scaling down of the use of nonviolent direct action in favour of less confrontational methods. Yet now, youth activists have begun to revitalize civil disobedience as a major form of action to unmask and confront not only global governing insti-*tutions like the WTO, IMF and World Bank, but also the corporate power structures that lie behind governments.*

From Mahatma Gandhi to Martin Luther King Jr., exercising resistance through civil disobedience must also be based on clear moral and political principles. After all, mobilizing people to disobey the established order calls for the assertion of an alternative moral and political authority.

To be effective, however, the use of direct action tactics require well-trained and disciplined troops on the front lines. In addition to the philosophy of civil disobedience, there is a need to know the issues at the centre of the protest, as well as a wide range of nonviolent tactics that can be used to resist the on-slaught of police and/or military forces, and to deal with potential arrest and imprisonment. U.S.-based groups like the Direct Action Network and the Ruckus Society have developed specialized training camps for youth activists in the art of civil disobedience. So, too, have groups like Opération SalAMI in Montreal and transAction in Toronto. In an article entitled "How We Really Shut Down the WTO" in Seattle, Starhawk, a California-based activist, described some of the key elements of direct action as follows:

"The participants in the action were organized into small groups called affinity groups. Each group was empowered to make its own decisions around how to participate in the blockade...Affinity groups were organized into clusters. The area around the Convention Center was broken down into 13 sections, and affinity groups and clusters committed to hold particular sections. As well, some groups were 'flying groups'—free to move to wherever they were most needed. All of this was co-ordinated at Spokescouncil meetings, where affinity groups each sent a representative who was empowered to speak for the group...

When faced with tear gas, pepper spray, rubber bullets, and horses, groups and individuals could assess their own ability to withstand the brutality. As a result, blockade lines held in the face of incredible police violence...No centralized leader could have coordinated the scene in the midst of the chaos, and none was needed: the organic, autonomous organization we had proved far more powerful and effective...The affinity groups, clusters, spokescouncils and working groups involved with the Direct Action Network (DAN) made decisions by consensus—a process that allows every voice to be heard and that stresses respect for minority opinions. We did not interpret consensus to mean unanimity. The only mandatory agreement was to act within the nonviolent guidelines. Beyond that, the DAN organizers set a tone that valued autonomy and freedom over conformity, and stressed co-ordination rather than pressure to conform.

The action included art, dance, celebration, cong, ritual and magic. It was more than a protest; it was an uprising of a vision of true abundance, a celebration of life and creativity and connection, that remained joyful in the face of brutality and brought live the creative forces that can truly counter those of injustice and control."

H. Culture Jamming

One of the most effective tools of action that youth activists have been able to use in building resistance to McWorld has been the art of "culture jamming." These tools emphasize two key factors: a) making creative use of the symbols of popular culture, and b) ensuring that the process is interactive and participatory. One style of culture jamming, for example, has been Michael Moore's recipe of mixing humour, satire, and ridicule. What Moore does is to enable people to think, laugh, and get angry at the same time about what big business and its CEOs are doing to people in everyday life. Another style has been developed by *Adbusters* magazine, where the aim has been to beat corporate advertisers at their own game. By getting artists, activists, educators and entertainers to produce "anti-ads," "subvertisements" and "uncommercials" opposing the ads placed by corporations in publications and on billboards, *Adbusters* uses "culture jamming" techniques to "uncool" the million-dollar images in corporate ads.

Anti-sweatshop campaigns have become one of the prime vehicles for the creative use of culture jamming tactics in the struggle against corporate globalization. Led by groups like the Campaign for Labor Rights and the National Labor Committee in the U.S., the Labour Behind the Label Coalition in the U.K., and unions like UNITE!, activists have used culture jamming to publicly expose the shameful exploitive labour practices by brand name corporations. By tackling the logo, label or icon that makes these corporations household names, campaign activists create a head-on collision between image and reality. At a 1999 protest rally against Disney, for example, participants parked a giant rubber rat outside a major Disney store. Similarly, at a New York rally launching "The Holiday Season of Conscience," speakers indicted Nike and Disney for their cheap labour practices in front of a giant red swoosh, along with 3-D displays of the Lion King.

In producing and promoting a documentary film called "Mickey Mouse Goes To Haiti," anti-sweatshop activist Charlie Kernaghan uses culture jamming techniques to expose Disney's cheap labour practices. Shown in high schools and campuses all over the U.S., Kernaghan's video applies some creative number-crunching to dramatize the contradictions between Disney's public image and its overseas operations. While Disney CEO Michael Eisner earns $9,783 an hour, for example, the average hourly wage of a Haitian worker is 28 cents. It would take a Haitian worker 16.8 years, says Kernaghan, to earn Eisner's salary income at Disney. What's more, the $181 million in stock options exercised by Eisner at Disney in 1996 is enough to provide for Disney's 19,000 Haitian workers and their families for 14 years.

When 1995-6 was designated by campaign activists as the Year of the Sweatshop, culture jamming was further used to tarnish the logos and images of brand name corporations through media stories exposing their exploitive labour practices. Major media outlets like 60 Minutes, 20/20, and the *New York Times* carried these stories. During this campaign year, talk show host Kathie Lee's sportswear line at Wal-Mart was publicly disclosed as being made by child labour in Honduras and by illegal sweatshops in the U.S. Here in Canada, the Maquila Soli-

darity Network has played a key role in exposing cheap labour practices of brand name corporations and reinforcing the fight for workers' rights in Central America by conducting sweatshop fashion shows across the country.

Increasingly, these and other kinds of culture jamming tactics are being used by youth activists in building resistance to the corporate advertising that now dominates life in universities, colleges, and high schools. Popular theatre is also being revived as a medium for communicating political humour, satire, and ridicule in ways that can be interactive and participatory. Sweatshop fashion shows are performed, along with survival games like 'transnational capital auction.' By involving drama students in colleges and schools, creative use is being made of street theatre for culture jamming purposes, not only in educational institutions, but in the community at large as well.

I. Building Alternatives

It is not enough, however, to organize campaigns of resistance to corporate domination alone. While the politics of resistance is a crucial component of youth struggles for social change today, there is also a need to anchor these actions in a vision of hope for the future. If youth are going to take control over their economic, social, and ecological future, there is a need to be conscious that one is fighting **for** something. In other words, it is important to be able to say "Yes" as well as "No," to affirm as well as to resist.

Yet, for far too long, we have all been fed an ongoing dosage of TINA—**T**here **I**s **N**o **A**lternative. Especially, ever since the collapse of the Berlin Wall and the end of the Cold War, big business and their government allies have been proclaiming that there is no alternative to global capitalism. This TINA syndrome, however, is nothing less than intellectual terrorism. It's also rooted in the politics of fear. The name of the game is to sap people's imaginations by scaring them into thinking that there really are no alternative ways of organizing the economy to serve the fundamental needs of people and the planet.

The fact is that There **A**re **T**housands of **A**lternatives—TATA—blooming in various forms all over the world. Many of these alternatives have to do with building a post-corporate society. The problem is that most people don't know these alternatives exist. The only way that people are going to know that viable alternatives do exist is to make them a vital part of public discussion and debate about key issues through campaigns. More importantly, there is a need to instill confidence in people that they can exercise their imaginative capacities and develop real alternatives.

Where people have taken these initiatives, they have done so by acting as if they are self-governing peoples. After all, being self-governing peoples is the essence of democracy. Whether, as youth activists, you are engaged in struggles for social change on the campus, in school, or in the community, or whether you are working on national or international campaign issues, it is important to act as self-governing peoples by defining and developing a viable agenda for transformation.

Take, for example, the need to develop new rules for governing both corporate donations and corporate advertising on university and college campuses. Why leave this task to the administration or the board of governors alone? There is no reason why students should not take the lead in drafting their own set of regulations, promoting campus-wide discussion and debate of these alternative rules, and demanding that they be adopted by the administration and the board of governors. Through groups like the Canadian Federation of Students, campaigns waged on one campus could be linked with those on other campuses. Similarly, there is no reason why high school students could not become involved in developing a set of guidelines or rules for governing business-school partnerships, organizing campaigns to build support for such alternative rules among parents, teachers, and the community at large.

Youth activists could also take the lead in developing an alternative budget for the running of their university, college or school. In doing so, insights could be drawn from the annual citizen-based budget-making process that goes on at federal, provincial and municipal levels. Each year, for example, the Canadian Centre for Policy Alternatives and CHO!CES (a Manitoba-based citizens' network) coordinate a process which brings together people from a variety of civil society organizations across Canada to participate in the development of what is called the *Alternative Fed-*

eral Budget (AFB). The AFB process involves a broad spectrum of sectors, including workers, women, farmers, consumers, environmentalists, religious, community and international development networks. Each sectoral organization identifies, in consultation with its membership, program priorities along with budget targets. Through an inter-sectoral negotiating process, budget priorities and targets are set. A technical team then does the necessary number-crunching and tests the feasibility of the proposals. After several months of consultation, negotiation and revisions, a peoples' *Alternative Federal Budget* is finalized and published.

Similar kinds of popular budget-making projects have also been initiated on a yearly basis in several provinces and municipalities across Canada. After all, budget-making is perhaps the most political activity of governing institutions in terms of setting and implementing priorities. In Brazil, the city of Porto Alegre has taken this process several steps further. Since 1989, a new model of governance has been instituted in the city of Porto Alegre which directly involves citizens in popular budget planning. Each year, hundreds of thousands of people participate in citizen forums organized in the 16 political jurisdictions of the city. Here, community-based priorities for government programs and investment are set, and citizen representatives are elected to participate in the final budget planning decisions. Through this democratic, particpatory process, citizens have learned what it means to be self-governing peoples.

New methods for developing citizen-based alternatives are also taking place elsewhere. In Chile, for example, social justice and environmental groups have led the way in developing a national plan for reorganizing their economy, called "Sustainable Chile." The plan was put together on the basis of community-based consultations that took place over a two-year period with workers and citizen activists in key sectors of the Chilean economy.

In 1999, the Brazilian state of Grand de Sol launched a new model of democratic governance by developing mechanisms for direct citizen participation in setting and monitoring public program priorities in healthcare, education, social services, community housing, ecological conservation, energy alternatives, industrial planning, economic investment, and public security. And here in Canada, the Council of Canadians' "Citizens'

Agenda" offers a similar process for pursuing economic and social transformation on local, national, and international fronts.

At the same time, the International Forum on Globalization has taken the lead in organizing ways of building alternatives to economic globalization. The IFG has prepared a discussion paper containing proposals and strategies for transforming the major institutions of global economic governance like the WTO, the IMF, and the World Bank, along with what needs to be done to make the United Nations the proper vehicle for governance at the international level. Called "Alternatives to Economic Globalization," the IFG document also includes alternative platforms for international trade, finance, and investment. The IFG has started conducting a series of regional conferences and teach-ins on every continent to promote discussion and debate on these alternatives, as well as to stimulate input and feedback based on local experiences. Steps are being taken to encourage active youth participation in this IFG initiative.

Taken together, these are some of the methods and strategies that could be further developed by youth activists in building movements of resistance and alternatives to McWorld.

Resource Materials:

Barlow, Maude, and Tony Clarke. *Global Showdown: How the New Activists are Fighting Global Corporate Rule.* Stoddart Books, Toronto, 2001.

Brecher, Jeremy, Tim Costello and Brendan Smith, *Globalization From Below: The Power of Solidarity.* South End Press, Cambridge, MA, 2000.

Hines, Colin, *Localization: A Global Manifesto.* Earthbound Publications Ltd., London and Sterling, 2000.

International Forum on Globalization, *Alternatives to Economic Globalization.* IFG Publications. San Francisco.

Klein, Naomi, *No Logo: Taking Aim at the Brand Bullies.* Alfred A. Knopf Canada, Toronto, 2000.

Klein, Naomi, "The Vision Thing," *The Nation,* 2001.

Rebick, Judy, *Imagine Democracy.* Stoddart Books, Toronto, 2000.

ACTIVITIES & WORKSHOPS
FOR ACTION

How are You Connected to the Global Economy?

(Developed with Karl Flecker)

Objective: *To identify the relationships that exist between our lives and globalization.*

Materials: Large world map, markers, paper, Ball of yarn/string.

The Approach: Ask participants to introduce themselves, telling a bit about themselves, if they have a job, where they're from, etc.

Ask participants to use the string to literally connect a good or service that they use or have within their daily lives in their community to another part of the map where they have a connection.

Have participants explain the relationship that exists for them between the spots they have linked as they make the connections. (e.g., My name is Jane and I live in Leamington. My family operates a family farm and the tomatoes produced on our farm are for export...My name is Dan and I live in Winnipeg. This morning for breakfast I ate fruit imported from the Dominican Republic and drank coffee from Colombia.)

Ask the group to stand up and form a circle and offer the following instructions to group:
As I read the following statements and, if true for you, take one step forward towards the centre, look to see who is with you, then step back.

Step forward if you:
... have disposable money for a job, allowances.
... know that as a worker you have basic rights.
... pay rent.
... have bills to pay. (What kind of bills?)
... are planning to go to university or college.
... know someone who has lost their job because of 'globalization.'
... are wearing an article of clothing that was made overseas.
... ate something this morning that was imported into Canada.
... knows someone who works for a corporation that employs people in
     more than one country. (Examples.)
... thinks that corporations have increasing political, economic power.
... have heard about the World Trade Organization. (What have you heard?)
... feel there are connections between government cuts, the global
     economy, and increasing poverty.

Talking Points:
These activities help demonstrate how much common ground we share with each other and with other communities around the world.
A lot of differences also exist; the economy can affect us in similar and conflicting way, i.e., the global economy brings us cheap clothes, pays wages, and can also take away jobs, our ability to run our own governments, and even threaten our health and the environment.

Roadmap to the Global Economy

(Developed with Karl Flecker)

Objectives:
1. To understand some of the basics about the various international structures, institutions and organizations that influence our lives.
2. To appreciate the short history these organizations have had.
3. To identify who and where opponents to corporate globalization can be found.

Materials:
A world map (for the 'road map')
Set of Trade Society Cards and Civil Society Cards (See attached).

The Approach:
Begin the activity by explaining you want participants to recall any significant event that may have happened in their lives, their community, or internally, for certain years you are going to call out.

After a few responses for the first year (see list and cards), share with the group the who, what, and when information for the Trade Society card for that year, and place it on the appropriate spot on the world map.

Proceed through all the Trade Society cards, getting one or two significant events from different participants for each card. Before proceeding to the Civil Society card, refer to the talking points.

Ask participants who and where they could find the alternatives to corporate globalization. Put the civil society cards on the map.

Alternatively, this activity can be done by using coloured paper/post-it notes: one colour for the Trade Society and another for the Civil Society. This enables participants to include additional organizations, groups, institutions, to the map.

Discussion Starters:
1. What do you notice about the map?
2. What kinds of changes might occur if the civil society organizations had the same kind of monetary and political resources as the Trade Society organizations?
3. What other organizations, groups, campaigns could be added to the map?

Talking Points:
Emphasize that these structures of corporate globalization have had a very short life span and that their history is very much connected to significant events in our own lives. Point out that in some cases—e.g., the Rubik's Cube, the Smurfs, and the TV show Miami Vice—pre-date some of these structures and they did not last that long. Change is possible!

Despite the size and apparent complexity of corporate globalization, their agenda is running into problems, not just because of the street protests, but because some of their internal plans are just bad business, incurring resistance from some of the corporate players.

The Civil Society Cards represent critical voices of dissent to the corporate agenda. The presence of this resistance movement worldwide is essential to our collective ability to confront corporate globalization.

Trade Society Cards represent the institutions and organizations that are driving the agenda of economic globalization forward.

Civil Society Cards represent the voices opposing and resisting the agenda of economic globalization.

* Note: The Trade Society Cards and Civil Society Cards are examples; there are several other organizations that could be included as well.

Trade Society Cards

North American Free Trade Agreement (NAFTA)

What: An agreement that eliminates barriers to trade among the three partners. It also seeks to eliminate barriers to investment and grants greater power to corporations.
Where: Signed between Canada, Mexico and the United States.
When: 1994

General Agreement on Tariffs and Trade (GATT)

What: The foremost series of trade agreements among nations.
Where: Morocco
When: 1947
Originally signed by 23 nations following the Second World War, many more countries signed on over the years. For decades this agreement covered nearly 90% of world trade among nearly 100 countries. Through various complex negotiations that spanned several years the GATT liberalized trade by removing tariff and non-tariff barriers.

World Bank

What: Funds roads, dams, and power plants and restructures the economies of the 'South'
Where: Washington DC
When: 1994
An international lending institution that manages $200 billion used to fund projects which are designed to integrate developing countries into the wider world economy. The World Bank requires countries receiving loans to implement Structural Adjustment Programs (SAPs). These programs are designed to make countries more competitive in the global market.

World Trade Organization (WTO)

What: Supersedes the GATT, writes and enforces economic rules that give corporations power over governments.
Where: Geneva
When: 1995
An 'economic constitution' that emerged from the GATT and functions as the global code of trade rules which primarily benefits corporations. The agreement administers and enforces international agreements (including agreements on agriculture, services, food safety and genetically modified organisms, intellectual property rights, investment, barriers to trade and dispute settlement). The fundamental difference between the GATT and the WTO is in the enforcement mechanisms. The WTO creates a global corporate government, not just a constitution or guidelines for countries.

International Monetary Fund

What: Provides governments with loans to help in times of credit problems.
Where: Washington DC
When: 1994

An international institution that provides loans to countries that are experiencing financial problems. The IMF offers loans on the condition of Structural Adjustment Programs (SAPs).

Free Trade Agreement (FTA)

What: An agreement signed between Canada and the United States to further liberalize trade of goods and services and deregulate the movement of capital.
When: 1988

Civil Society Cards

Jubilee 2000

What: An international campaign, based on the Biblical tradition which calls for a Jubilee year every 50 years, when slaves are set free and debts cancelled;
calling for the cancellation of the unpaid debts of the world's poorest countries without conditions that will further harm people living in poverty or the environment.
Where: worldwide campaigns - Cameroon, Canada, Ethiopia, Europe, Honduras, India, Nicaragua, The Philippines, South Africa, United Kingdom, USA among many more
When: The cancellation of debts by 2000.

The Council of Canadians

What: An independent, non-partisan citizens' interest group which organizes campaigns on issues including international trade, genetic engineering, water and healthcare. The Council of Canadians was at the forefront in the struggle to defeat the Multilateral Agreement on Investment in 1998.
Where: Headquartered in Ottawa, regional organizers and local chapters across the country.
When: 1985

Third World Network

What: One of the world's leading voices in opposition to present corporate globalization, working primarily with activists in Asia, Africa and South America, linking with other organizations from the North.
Where: Malaysia
When: early 1980s

Maquila Solidarity Network

What: A Canadian network promoting solidarity with groups in Mexico, Central America and Asia organizing in maquiladora factories and export-processing zones to improve conditions and win a living wage as well as work together for employment with dignity, fair wages and working conditions. The MSN has been instrumental in establishing and supporting the Students Against Sweatshop campaigns in high schools and on campuses across Canada.
Where: office in Toronto
When: 1995

Zapatistas

What: Indigenous people in Mexico who rebelled against 500 years of oppression. The rebellion coincided with the signing of NAFTA by the governments of Canada, Mexico and the USA. Their rebellion brought to the fore conditions of poverty, hunger, landlessness that the indigenous of the world suffer.
Where: Chiapas, Mexico
When: The rebellion began on January 1, 1994.

50 Years is Enough

What: A broad-based coalition working for global economic justice. The network is committed to making international financial institutions like the World Bank and International Monetary Fund more democratic and accountable to the people impacted by the institutions' policies.
Where: Washington DC
When: 1994, on the 50-year anniversary of the establishment of the World Bank and IMF.

The Clothes on Your Back

(Developed with Karl Flecker)

Objectives:
1. To reinforce personal connections to the global economy.
2. To raise issues of human rights and workers' rights within the global, corporate economic system.

Materials: World map, Post-it notes, and pens/pencils for participants, Wage card (below)

The Approach:

Inform the group that this short activity will illustrate how we are all personally connected to the global economy literally by the clothes on our backs. It helps us to understand who is benefiting the most from the global, corporate economic system, and who is paying for it.

This activity also illustrates how the corporate global trade agenda relies on racism, sexism, and disregard for workers' rights in order to maximize profit margins.

Instruct participants to pair up, introduce themselves, and check the label on an article of clothing of your partner to see where it came from. Jot down the origin on a Post-it note. When the pairs have finished, have one of each pair come to the map and place the Post-it note on the appropriate spot on the world map.

Wage Card
Hourly base or starting wage in the apparel industry (U.S. dollars).

USA	$8.42
Canada	$6.70
Philippines	$0.62
El Salvador	$0.60
Mexico	$0.54
Honduras	$0.43
China	$0.30
Nicaragua	$0.25
Indonesia	$0.22
India	$0.20
Bangladesh	$0.17

Source: *Wages, Benefits, Poverty Line and meeting Workers need in the Apparel and Footwear Industries of Selected Countries*, U.S. Dept. of Labor, Feb. 2000.

When the pairs have finished, ask the group what they notice about the map: i.e., where is production concentrated. Ask the group to imagine what the workers are like who made their clothes. Ask what they know or imagine might be their working conditions.

Add these points if they have not been made by the group:
The typical garment worker is a woman, likely a young woman from the countryside, with little education or experience of unions or organizing. This is the "skill set" or profile factory managers look for. The worker is likely a person of colour, no matter if the garment shop is abroad or in Canada or the U.S.

Refer to the Maquila Solidarity Network's wage card (above) to examine how much the worker earns to produce the clothes sold in retail stores across North America. How do the workers' wages compare with the cost of the garment that we pay in stores?

Corporate Tours

Objectives:
1. To unmask the trail of corporate power that influences our lives.
2. To make concrete abstract concepts of corporate power.
3. To "out" various corporations and corporate leaders.
4. To get out of the workshop in a room format and have some fun.

Materials: pen, paper, tour guides, map

The Approach:

Review the objectives that you are hoping to achieve with the tour. Are there particular themes you want to focus on? Who are your targets?

Your first step in preparing for the tour is to gather the research and information about your particular targets. The following are some broad questions you might want to answer in compiling your information for the tour:

What is your target's relationship to the campus, community or school? How do they participate in the campus, community or school?

What is the corporate policy or track record on environmental, social, economic, labour issues?

Who is the CEO? How much do they earn (versus how much the workers earn)?

What are their profits? Do they pay their taxes?

Talking Points:

The concept of the corporate tours has been used in a variety of forms. In Toronto, local anti-corporate activists wanted to take folks to the doorsteps of the corporations and the homes of the CEOs that intimately influence our lives through their products, decisions and power. The idea also included putting a face on these seemingly invisible corporations. Tours could be designed in a close geographical area and conducted as a walking tour, or, if you have access to a bus or van, the tour could be taken on the road.

The tours can be done by individuals or as a group. If done as a group, members can take on different components of the research and the tour itself.

Are they involved in any disputes? Have organizations or groups targeted them (boycotts, etc.)?

What other information, facts, statistics would be helpful for the tour?

After you've compiled mini-profiles on the targets, you're ready to give the tour! You'll probably have a lot of information to share along the tour, and it may be helpful to design a tour guide for participants that would include some of the information you'll share. (See a sample tour guide on next page.)

Corporate Bus Tour

Bechtel Canada Co., 12 Concorde Place, Toronto

Bechtel Canada Co., a subsidiary of the Bechtel Group, is an engineering-construction organization, working on more than 19,000 projects in 140 nations. Bechtel has worked on projects including constructing the Hoover Dam, the James Bay Hydroelectric. In 1998, Bechtel won a contract from the World Bank to privatize the water services in Bolivia's third largest city, Cochabamba. Water prices more than doubled after Bechtel came in. After four months of uprising and struggle by the people of Bolivia, Bechtel was forced out. Bechtel is now demanding a $12 million compensation package from the Bolivian government for breaking the contract.

Nike, 110 Bloor Street West, Toronto

Nike is the market leader in the sports footwear industry, with approximately 37% of the market. Nike has responded to pressure about the health & safety standards, working conditions and wages raised by numerous groups, however it's important to keep the pressure on them. Nike CEO Phil Knight received 5,273 times the annual pay of the average worker in a Nike shoe factory in 1998. Labour production for a pair of Nike running shoes accounts for only 4% of the cost! If Nike cut 4% from its worldwide marketing outlay, it could provide a living wage to all of its Indonesian workers. This could hardly affect its profits.

Loblaws, 22 St. Clair Avenue East, Toronto

Loblaws, part of the Galen Weston empire, has recently been targeted for the genetically engineered ingredients in their products which are not labelled. It is estimated that between 60-75% of all prepackaged food in Canada contains GE ingredients. Loblaws President Choice products are the biggest label in Canada, meaning every time we buy a product we're potentially buying a lot of GE substances we're not aware are there. Loblaws has opposed mandatory labelling of genetically engineered food.

McDonald's Corporation, 1 McDonald Place, Toronto

Since McDonald's opened in the 1950s, the number of restaurants has ballooned to over 26,000 restaurants in 119 countries worldwide. Second to Santa Claus, the McDonald's 'golden arches' are the world's most recognizable image. In 1999, McDonald's served 3 million Canadians and over 43 million worldwide everyday.

Shell Canada Inc., 90 Sheppard Avenue West, Toronto

Shell Canada is part of Royal Dutch, an international petroleum company. Shell/Royal Dutch began drilling in Nigeria in 1958 and has drilled an estimated 900 million barrels of oil worth billions of dollars since that time. Between 1982 and 1992, independent sources estimate that 1,626,000 gallons of Shell oil were spilled in Nigerian land. The operations have been disastrous for the people of Nigeria. Shell has been condemned for its role in Nigeria in terms of the devastation of the environment, and the human rights abuses that have continued at the expense of the Ogoni people.

Welcome to Queen's...the Corporate Campus

Post secondary education is up for sale! Price tags attached to everything from individual programs to the knowledge we learn to students ourselves. There has always been a business element to universities and colleges, but the involvement of the private sector has become much more entrenched in the last 20 years. Corporations are now in the drivers' seats and universities and colleges and post secondary education is being fundamentally transformed from a public system what is built on autonomy, pursues knowledge and truth and is accessible and affordable.

Corporate Governance and Corporate Fundraising, Summerhill

The Queen's University Board of Trustees make the decisions that directly impact students. They have voted for tuition fee increases, privatizing programs and are now pursuing deregulation. The Board includes, Peter Lougheed, Queen's Chancellor, former Alberta premier and representative to numerous corporate boards. Thomas O'Neill, Chief Operating Officer of PriceWaterhouseCoopers Global, John Rae, Exec. V.P. Power Corporation and fundraiser for the Chrétien Liberals.

Queen's University has aggressively pursued fundraising. Melvin Goodes, former Board of Trustees member and former Chairman and CEO of Warner-Lambert contributed $10 million toward a new building for the School of Business. $11 million was contributed toward a new Chemistry building by the Chernoff Family. DuPont Canada contributed $2.5 million toward the creation of the DuPont Chair in Engineering Education Research and Development within the Faculty of Applied Science.

Commercialized Research: BioSciences Complex

This $52.5 million building houses a number of faculties as well as spin off companies. PARTEQ Innovations is Queen's technology transfer office. The corporation where partnerships with the private sector as fostered and research, knowledge commercialized. Since it was established in 1987, 17 spin off companies have been facilitated through their offices. Performance Plants, Nanometals Corporation are also housed within the BioSciences Complex.

Dishonourable Mention goes to the **Queen's School of Business** for having the first privatized MBA program in Canada. Corporate funders to the School of Business include: Warner-Lambert, Scotiabank, Nortel, Proctor & Gamble and Andersen Consulting.

Pension Fund Investments: Talisman Energy

The consortium of oil producers led by Talisman in Sudan includes companies from China, Malaysia and Sudan. Drilling from existing wells in the Greater Nile Oil Project began two years ago, followed by the establishment of processing plants and the construction of the pipeline. By the summer of 1999, oil was flowing through the pipeline to Port Sudan for export. With goals of producing 150,000 barrels a day, Talisman provides oil free of charge to the Sudanese government, thereby allowing other revenues to be used to finance the civil war. As of last spring, Queen's University had $2.7 million invested in Talisman. The endowment investments were withdrawn however the pension plan funds remain.

Sodexho-Marriott Services, Ban Righ Cafeteria

Sodexho-Marriott Services is the largest institutional food services provider in North America, generating $4.5 billion in annual revenues and has signed exclusive food agreements with many Canadian universities including a contract that has been in place at Queen's for 25 years. Sohexho-Marriott uses the profits generated by students to support private prisons. Sodexho-Marriott has holding in Corrections Corporation of America, the world's largest for-profit prison company. Unwittingly, students of the more than 400 campuses served by Marriott's are being dragged into the company's poor judgement.

always **Coca-Cola** ...
Queen's University recently jumped into the cola wars being waged on North American university and college campuses by signing a 10 year exclusive contract with Coca-Cola.

Linkages

Objective:
1. To identify the connections between the issues that impact our lives.

Materials: Markers, flip chart paper, lots of yarn, chairs.

Discussion Starters:
What were some of the ideas generated during the first brainstorming session?

Are there connections between the two different issues?

What are the connections?

If connections are made between the two issues, the groups with the yarn will loop the yarn around the leg of the chair, and then with the entire group rotate again.

The groups travelling with the ball of yarn will always use their original issue during the brainstorming at each new chair they visit.

Once the groups have rotated past all the chairs, the rotating groups will return to their original chairs. With the entire group at the chair, share some of the linkages made.

The Approach:

Prior to beginning the activity, set up the room (or large open space) with chairs forming a large circle. The number of chairs should correspond with the number of small groups into which the one large group will be divided for the activity.

At each chair, tie one end of a ball of yarn to the chair leg, leaving the ball of yarn beside the chair on the floor.

For example: If you are working with a group of 32 participants, you could place 8 chairs in a circle and ask participants to form smaller groups of 4 at each chair.

Also, leave a piece of flip chart paper and a marker at each chair. At the top of each piece of flip chart paper write down an issue. (Suggestions and ideas are listed below.)

Homelessness, youth, education, globalization, consumerism, poverty, food, sweatshops, governments, corporations, the arts, environment, urban, rural, employment, technology.

Divide the large group into smaller groups. (Depending on the size of the large group, the activity works well with small groups of between 2-4 people.)

Once participants have settled at their chair, ask the groups to spend a couple of minutes brainstorming all of the words, ideas, concepts, etc., they can think of relating to the issue written on their flip chart.

After a few minutes, ask half of the group at the chair to take the yarn attached to the leg of the chair and rotate to a new chair.

At the new chair, the participants who have rotated to a new chair will brainstorm with the original group members who have not moved, trying to find connections between the two issues.

Report back/debriefing...

What were some of the issues you identified at your original chair?

As you rotated, what did you discover?

Were there connections that you had not thought of before?

What are some of the things we can take from this activity?

Twenty Questions: Test Your Globalization Trivia

1. Wal-Mart has more economic clout than how many countries?
A) 163
B) 148
C) 101 D) 48

2. Which countries hold the majority of power at the World Trade Organization?
A) Australia, European Union, Japan, USA
B) EU, Japan, Russia, USA
C) Canada, European Union, Japan, USA
D) Australia, EU, NZ, USA

3. Which corporate symbol is the most recognized image worldwide?
A) Mickey Mouse, Disney
B) The Golden Arches, McDonald's
C) Swoosh, Nike
D) IMAC, MacIntosh

4. What year was the World Trade Organization established?
A) 1947
B) 1981
C) 1995
D) 1999

5. Which individual has more wealth than the combined Gross National Products of Guatemala, El Salvador, Costa Rica, Panama, Nicaragua, Belize, Jamaica and Bolivia?
A) George Soros
B) Michael Jordan
C) Britney Spears
D) Bill Gates

6. How much money circulates electronically every day as part of the global financial casino?
A) $7.9 billion
B) $2 trillion
C) $3.4 trillion
D) $10.1 trillion

7. How many countries are involved in the negotiations of the Free Trade Area of the Americas (FTAA) (an agreement that would create the largest trading bloc in the western hemisphere)?
A) 24
B) 29
C) 34
D) 41

8. How much of the world's population workers do the world's top 200 transnational corporations employ?
A) less than 1%
B) 2%
C) 5%
D) 9%

9. What is the hourly base wage in the apparel industry for Nicaraguan workers?
A) $0.25
B) $0.80
C) $1.10
D) $3.50

10. What is the estimated percentage of pre-packaged food that contains genetically modified substances?
A) 15%
B) 45%
C) 75%
D) 95%

11. How much is the World Bank's total portfolio worth?
A) $750 million
B) $200 billion
C) $900 billion
D) $1 trillion

12. How many business school partnerships exist in Canada?
A) less than 1,000
B) 7,000
C) 13,000
D) more than 20,000

13. Of the 12.5 minutes of the Youth News Network, how many minutes are advertising?
A) 1 minute
B) 2.5 minutes
C) 5 minutes
D) 7.5 minutes

14. What does the acronym GATS stand for?
A) General Agreement on Trade Secrets
B) General Acquisition of Total Services
C) Great Attack on Trade in Services
D) General Agreement on Trade in Services

15. How many transnational corporations are there worldwide?
A) over 44,000
B) 38,000
C) 23,000
D) less than 10,0000

16. Which two transnational corporations hosted the Seattle WTO Ministerial in December 1999?
A) Monsanto & Pfizer
B) Exxon & Philip Morris
C) Merrill Lynch & General Motors
D) Boeing & Microsoft

17. How much is spent on military weapons and operations worldwide every year?
A) $1 trillion
B) $780 billion
C) $25 billion
D) $900 million

18. Of the Top 200 corporations, what percentage of the total workforce is employed by Wal-Mart?
A) 0.5%
B) 1%
C) 2.5%
D) 5%

19. Of the top 200 corporations, how many are American?
A) 42
B) 51
C) 70
D)82

20. The CEO's from which two Canadian corporations established the Business Council on National Issues?
A) Royal Bank of Canada & Eaton's
B) Petro Canada & Power Corporation
C) Hollinger & CIBC
D) Imperial Oil & Noranda

Answers:
1. A, 2. C, 3. B, 4. C, 5. D, 6. B, 7. C, 8. A, 9. A, 10. C, 11. B, 12. D, 13. B, 14. D, 15. A, 16. D 17. B, 18. C, 19. D, 20. D

Alphabet Soup	Movers & Shakers	McSchool	Globalize This!	Beyond McWorld
What is the North American Free Trade Agreement (NAFTA)?	What are Transnational Corporations (TNCs)?	What is $7 Billion?	What are France, Germany, Japan, the Netherlands and the United States?	What is solidarity?
What is the Free Trade Area of the Americas (FTAA)?	What is the Business Council on National Issues (BCNI)?	What are private universities?	What are sweatshops?	What is fair trade?
What is the World Trade Organization (WTO)?	What is the World Economic Forum (WEF)?	What are Coca Cola and Pepsi?	Who is Bill Gates?	What are Human Rights?
What is the International Monetary Fund (IMF)?	What is the Fraser Institute?	What are business school partnerships?	What are Genetically Modified Organisms (GMOs)?	What is democracy?
What is the General Agreement on Trade in Services (GATS)?	What is the global financial casino?	What is the Youth News Network (YNN)?	What are McDonald's Golden Arches?	What is sustainability?

Alphabet Soup	Movers & Shakers	McSchool	Globalize This!	Beyond McWorld
The government of United States, Canada & Mexico signed the agreement in 1994. This deal provides unregulated trade between these countries & curtails governments abilities to protect citizens or moderate corporate behaviour.	These private companies are active in the global economy & operate in many countries. They also wield tremendous political and social power.	Since the Liberal government came to power in 1993, equalization/transfer payments for post-secondary education to the provinces have been cut by this amount.	90% of TNCs are headquartered in these five industrial countries.	These actions, campaigns, and spirit, support people's movements and campaigns fighting for justice in other communities and countries.
This agreement extends the North American Free Trade Agreement to 34 countries in North, Central & South America (excluding Cuba) creating one trading bloc affecting nearly 1 billion people.	A Canadian pro-business lobby group that was created in 1975. The CEOs from the 150 largest corporations sit at this table. They have combined revenues of $500 billion, control assets of $1.9 trillion & have a workforce of 1.4 million employees. To join, membership fees are a steep $50,000 a year.	These institutions sell a post-secondary education for profit, have poor working conditions, lousy pay, questionable benefits and accessibility are not always a part of the degree. Students assume the full cost of their education.	Garment factories that often have poor working conditions, lousy pay, questionable benefits and dominated principally by young children & women being exploited for less than a living wage.	This is a process that ensures fair and equitable wages for the producers of goods, recognizes the value of the product and the production of the product and is environmentally and socially sustainable.
This institution was established in 1995 to promote & enforce rules related to virtually all forms of trade amongst nations. It is based in Geneva, Switzerland but holds meetings around the world. Its membership is made up of 140 countries.	A club with 1000 of the world's CEOs from the largest corporations on the planet as well as international political figures & media pundits who are unabashed cheerleaders for an integrated global economy.	These two corporate giants are battling for monopolies on university/college campuses and in schools to satiate their thirst for profits.	A man whose wealth is greater than the combined gross national products of Guatemala, El Salvador, Costa Rica, Panama, Nicaragua, Belize, Jamaica, and Bolivia.	These are the basic rights entitled to all people including civil, political, economic, social, gender equality, cultural, etc.
This institution was created in 1944 to promote economic recovery & cooperation following the devastating affects of WWII. It provides loans to member countries & dictates strict conditions - 'structural adjustment programs' - as a condition of their loans. Invariably it is the poorest countries most severely affected.	A Canadian based think-tank that promotes free market ideology, privatization, deregulation, and such. This organization works hard to affect public policy development spin in the media to their point of view and engage young people in their research.	Usually unequal arrangements between a corporation and a school where cash is exchanged for a captive audience. There are over 20,000 of these arrangements in place across Canada.	These are the result of big business and science coming together to hasten nature's talents for their profit. They are estimated to be in 75% of all prepackaged food on shelves today.	This is a decision-making process whereby all people are able to govern themselves and fully participate.
This broad agreement being negotiated under the WTO & the new rules being developed, (mostly in secret) will apply to virtually every service.	More than $1.5 trillion flows across borders everyday as part of this.	This daily 12.5 minute video program requires schools to have their students view the 10 minutes of "news" and "current events" reporting, and 2.5 minutes of commercials as part of their in-class work.	This corporate symbol is the most recognized image worldwide.	This form of development meets needs without compromising or harming future generations abilities to meet their needs.

Alphabet Soup	Movers & Shakers	McSchool	Globalize This!	Beyond McWorld
$100	$100	$100	$100	$100
$200	$200	$200	$200	$200
$300	$300	$300	$300	$300
$400	$400	$400	$400	$400
$500	$500	$500	$500	$500

IMPRIMÉ AU CANADA